O F

KINGS

— AND —

PROPHETS

MARK RUTLAND

CHARISMA HOUSE

Visit the author's website at drmarkrutland.com.

Cataloging-in-Publication Data is on file with the Library of Congress.
International Standard Book Number: 978-1-62999-836-7
E-book ISBN: 978-1-62999-837-4

21 22 23 24 25 — 987654321
Printed in the United States of America

Table of Contents

Foreword

I F YOU ARE an avid reader and student of the Bible, you may have noticed at times that the Word of God presents themes and situations that are somewhat difficult to fully grasp. Even more concerning is how some can read meanings into God's Word that may not actually be there. This creates conflict and confusion within the body of Christ that is so far off from the unity God calls us to exhibit. However, in my many years of reading Scripture, I have observed that one of the reasons we do not understand—or we misinterpret—details of the New Testament is because we have an incomplete comprehension of what happened in the Old Testament. There is simply no way to fully appreciate the majesty of how God reveals Himself in the New Testament apart from digging into the roots of the Old Testament.

One area that appears to be particularly confusing these days is that of leadership and how we can relate to those in power. I am grateful that my friend Dr. Mark Rutland, who shares my profound love for God's Word, has taken the time to delve into the Old Testament and find answers to many of the questions believers are asking today. In his newest book, *Of Kings and Prophets*, Mark takes a unique look into the lives of Old Testament leaders and the holy men the Lord chose to speak through. His book is focused on the relationships between the men who sat on the thrones of Israel and Judah and the prophets of God who both rebuked and advised them. By examining their interactions, we are privy to insights into how Christians can and should hold leaders accountable. We also receive invaluable guidance about how we as believers can exemplify godly involvement in our churches, communities, and country.

Mark asks and answers the question, How can the church live up to its prophetic mandate if we care more about what politicians can do for the church than what Jesus demands of the church? The prophets fearlessly confronted the most powerful leaders of their day, the kings. They also comforted them, advised them, and when they strayed, guided them back to the Lord their God and Redeemer. As men and women called to serve Jesus in the body of Christ, we must "sanctify Christ as Lord in [our] hearts, always being ready to make a defense to everyone who asks [us] to give an account for the hope that is in [us], but with gentleness and respect."[1] We must live godly lives so we can look anyone we meet in the eye—whether in the church, in the marketplace, in adversarial circumstances, or in the halls of power—and lovingly lead them to the God of grace through the proclamation of the truth.

That's why studies of the kings and prophets are so crucial—because the prophets were God's holy messengers. They still speak to us today and show us how to be "ambassadors for Christ, as though God were making an appeal through us."[2]

It is my prayer that you will embrace the journey Mark is about to take you on and allow the prophets to speak to you as they spoke to kings. Get closer to these great Old Testament men of God, learn from them, glean from their wisdom, and let them shape you. Because as Proverbs instructs, "one who walks with wise people will be wise."[3] Not only will they show you how to stand before kings, but they will teach you how to represent the King of kings and bring glory to His name.

—Dr. Charles Stanley
Founder, In Touch Ministries
Pastor Emeritus, First Baptist Church of Atlanta

CHAPTER 1

The Counsel of God in the Muddle of Men

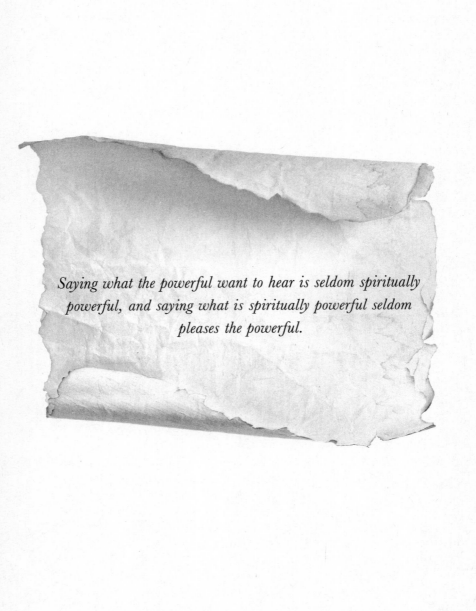

Saying what the powerful want to hear is seldom spiritually powerful, and saying what is spiritually powerful seldom pleases the powerful.

I N THE COURSE of a university lecture on, of all things, the nature of revival, I recounted some of the negative and positive results of the Welsh revival. I mentioned that despite some excesses and mistakes, 100,000 were converted in one year, missionaries were sent around the world, and the local society was deeply impacted for good. As one example, I offered the corroborating statistic that arrests for public drunkenness dropped by more than 50 percent in the first few weeks of the revival.

One student immediately raised her hand and angrily announced: "I haven't heard anything about this. Why isn't this on the news? Is the liberal press refusing to report this?"

I hardly knew what to say. I felt embarrassed for her, and I did not want to add to the awkwardness by making her feel foolish. I needn't have worried. "I'm sorry," I said. "I may not have made it clear. This happened in 1904 and 1905. I just assumed..."

"Well, good lands!" she cut me off. "Why are we talking about this at all? We don't care about a revival that happened in 1904! That's not why we attended this. Tell us about revival right now. Anything that happened in 1904 is irrelevant to us."

To be faithful and generous to her classmates, I'm not sure she spoke for all of them, though none of them rose to contradict her. They seemed instead to be waiting to see if I had an answer to what she obviously felt, and perhaps some of them felt as well, was the end of my credibility. I mean, 1904? Really?

I suggested to her that if a revival in Wales a mere 120 years ago was irrelevant, the Upper Room must have absolutely no meaning at all since it happened more than two thousand years ago. She reluctantly conceded the point, but only partially, claiming, "Well, the Bible is different." Indeed, it is.

Such dismissive chronocentrism as hers is unfortunate, to be sure. Some, however—and this is infinitely worse—make much the same argument about the Old Testament. They have a sort of "that was then, this is now" attitude toward Genesis through Malachi. They point out that the people in those books were ancient pre-Christian Jews who lived thousands of years ago. Why should our understanding of who Jesus is in life today have to be set against such an irrelevant backdrop? These people cannot seem to see, however, that the predictable extrapolation of this reasoning will be disastrous. A New Testament without the weight of an *Old* Testament seems to be what some are suggesting. The problem is that may lead inexorably to a non-biblical but highly contemporary Christianity free of the weight of that pesky, irrelevant *New* Testament. In other words, if we carve out the Old Testament, then why not the New Testament as well.

Unfortunately, even those not quite ready to jettison the entire Old Testament want to at least lighten its load by dropping some of it in favor of parts that seem more relevant. They say—or at least think—"What can Leviticus or Deuteronomy mean to us today?" They are often particularly dismissive of the prophets. Others are in favor of keeping the prophets but want to choose their prophets carefully—and often politically. These folks quote the prophets whose messages are in agreement with what they believe or will buttress their political argument.

That brings us to the purpose of this book. I did not want to write a biographical sketchbook of the prophets. Nor did I want to zero in on their messages. What I was after and what I hope you will receive is a fresh look at one particular aspect of the prophet's ministry: what happened when a prophet arrived at some intersection of history at the same time as one of the kings.

That flash point was what I wanted to explore.

The ridiculous quicksand of contemporary vocabulary has made it virtually impossible to use terms such as *truth* and *power*. It has become popular to speak "your truth" rather than *the* truth. Shouting down a speaker or hijacking a meeting by screaming obscenities at the opposite viewpoint is now called "speaking truth to power."

The prophets actually did speak truth to power. They spoke real truth, not some mulligan stew of popular causes, and they spoke it to real power, not some easily intimidated politician trying to get reelected. The prophets spoke to kings, real kings whose word was law and who could have ordered them executed in the blink of an eye. The prophets, though not perfect, were incredibly courageous. The kings were, well, human and therefore flawed. Their power was unchecked; therefore, their flaws were magnified. Some of the kings, such as Ahab, were idolatrous murderers. Others were merely unprincipled narcissists who despised being told the truth.

Some incredibly shallow but incredibly passionate movie star spouts the accepted party line relative to the cause of the hour, and she is hailed as courageous. Few seem inclined to point out that virtually everyone already agrees with her at the awards ceremony where she so fearlessly said what would make her even more popular with her colleagues. That is not speaking truth to power.

John the Baptist was the cousin of Jesus of Nazareth. He was by any reasonable definition a great prophet, a colossus who stood with one foot squarely in the Old Testament and the other in the New Testament. Not unlike his cousin Jesus, John was beloved by the masses and hated by the power brokers of his day. Surely the religious leaders of John's day were bound to be delighted at the tsunami of genuine repentance and holiness of life and heart. Surely those in positions of religious power would want the hearts of the people turned dramatically back toward God. Surely. However, all but the most naive know that was never going to be true. Those with the most religious power had the most to lose, and they were not going to surrender to some wild man waist-deep in the Jordan River. When John spoke to that mob, he spoke truth to power. They hated John the Baptist, but from Scripture it's unclear if they had the power or a robust plan to kill him.

Herod Antipas was a different matter. Herod needed no plan. All he had to do was snap his fingers. Herod Antipas was the puppet king of Israel, propped up on his throne by the sustaining might of Rome. His power was relatively local, but it was absolute. Herod Antipas was a dangerously weak, incestuous egomaniac and the son of Herod the Great, who was a genocidal, homicidal maniac.

John knew all this. He was not deluded. He was courageous. He called Herod Antipas out for his incestuous "marriage" to his own sister-in-law, the wife of his half-brother, Herod Philip. John denounced this wickedness in high places in no uncertain terms, and Herod immediately threw John in prison. John might have languished there or even been released had it not been for the hateful machinations of Herod's "wife," Herodias, and the erotic dance of her daughter. Herod was a lunatic from a family full of lunatics, but Herodias was not exactly Mother Teresa. She basically turned her own daughter into a porn star in order to see John the Baptist's head on a platter.

One preacher said John underestimated the fury of a woman publicly denounced for what she was. That is not true. John was not confused or naive. He was not some unsophisticated primitive who mistook how far he could go with impunity. He was a prophet, and he was courageous.

The Old Testament prophets were a rare breed, and their spiritual blood flowed in the veins of John the Baptist. The DNA of the prophets is powerful stuff, but it is not the key to popularity with ruthless power brokers.

What about John the Baptist? Was he really a prophet? Of course he was, and Jesus said he was, but was he a prophet like Elijah? His entire life story, as brief and tumultuous as it was, is recorded solely in the New Testament, so in that sense he was a New Testament prophet. However, he prophesied the immediate appearance of Messiah, which would make him the last of the Old Testament prophets, very like Isaiah, for example.

That leads to two questions: Were there other New Testament prophets? Are there still prophets today? As to the first question, yes. Agabus, for example, was a trusted prophet in the New Testament. In fact, he was one of a group of prophets described in the Book of Acts who came from Jerusalem to Antioch.[1] Agabus prophesied a great famine, and the church at Antioch, trusting that prophecy, immediately sent relief funds to the believers in Jerusalem. Agabus' prophecy is validated by a date stamp: "This [famine] took place in the reign of Claudius."[2] Suetonius, the Roman historian, records this famine as being so horrible and lasting so long—AD 44 to AD 48—that Roman mobs even threatened the emperor himself.[3]

The same Agabus appears again in Acts 21 to prophesy dramatically that if Paul the apostle returns to Jerusalem he will be arrested and handed over to the Gentile powers. Paul does not deny the validity of the prophecy. He simply says he is prepared to suffer and die. Paul does indeed go to Jerusalem, and every word of Agabus' prophecy comes true.

Therefore, we can safely say that John the Baptist was not the only New Testament prophet. Acts also records that Philip the evangelist had four virgin daughters "which did prophesy."[4] Luke, the writer of Acts, does not go so far as to call them prophets. He simply says that they did what prophets do. It may be a difference without a distinction, but the specific language is worth noting.

All of which brings us to today. Are there prophets today? This book is not about the gifts of the Spirit in the contemporary church. That is for another book. I have written and preached on that subject in the past, and I reserve the right to do so in the future, but here I want to deal only with prophecy.

Agabus, the fact that he existed and the church in his own time accepted him as a prophet, speaks loudly that there were New Testament prophets. There are no prophets today who are fully and widely accepted as prophets by the church at large, beyond some smaller enclave. That may speak to the disappearance of that office. Some will claim that. It may just speak to the spiritual poverty and splintered theological divisiveness of the contemporary community of faith. That also is for another book.

What I want to speak to is the true nature of prophets. Some modern "prophets" are really encouragers. Encouraging others with hopeful words, such as "your blessing is on the way" or "God will return all you've lost," is hardly a bad thing. I love to hear encouraging words, and saying them to others is a good ministry. However, unless it is a specific prophecy given to a prophet by God Himself—if the "prophet" is just lifting someone's spirits, if it is a general "word" tweeted out to the masses—we dare not call it a prophecy nor its author a prophet.

Neither of Agabus' recorded prophecies were positive. One was about a famine and one was about the impending arrest and imprisonment of the apostle Paul. This is not to say all valid prophecy must be negative. Hardly. A more positive prophecy than John the Baptist's words "Behold the lamb of God, which taketh away the sin of the world"[5] cannot be imagined.

It is, however, important to see that a constant stream of general feel-good statements do not a prophet make. Neither do emotionally driven "prophecies" about current events. For example, anyone who prophesies about specific front-page news must be held accountable. Prophets who "prophesy" what they hope will happen are not prophets at all. God is not obligated to fulfill the wish lists of preachers who claim prophetic authority. Preachers who claim prophetic authority are obligated to hear from God, say only what He says, add nothing, omit nothing, and then live or die with the consequences.

Prophets are seldom popular. Respected, yes. Popular, maybe not so much. My suspicion is that when Agabus showed up at a meeting, some in the back row headed for the parking lot. Prophets are rarely loved by those in positions of religious or political power.

Favor with those in high places can be a gift of God. It can also be a deadly and deadening trap. Saying what the powerful want to hear is seldom spiritually powerful, and saying what is spiritually powerful seldom pleases the powerful. The anointed word of God is a two-edged sword. The leaders of the present age are always nervous about swords in the hands of others, and they seldom treat prophets with respect.

When John the Baptist's mangled and headless corpse lay on the floor of Herod's prison and John's head was carried in on a platter, those at Herod's party laughed and rejoiced while heaven welcomed a prophet home. Herod and his friends sat in the seat of luxury and walked the halls of worldly power even as John entered the gates of glory.

The voice of prophecy will grow weak and confused when the church settles for celebrity and "access to the palace." Prophets care little for such things or even for the preservation of their own lives. They hear from God in the various lonely deserts of life and declare His word unalloyed to those who may least want to hear it.

The history of humanity is the story of power. It is power that nations strive to seize and may lose when they send their armies into the field. Power is the inner infection in every fevered night of domestic violence. Power is the salacious delight of the leering bully and the cold, desperate lack that grips the frightened victim. From the moment Cain took a stone and caved in his brother's skull, the poisonous lust for power has pulsed through the veins of fallen humanity.

After Cain came Nimrod. He was a mighty hunter—of men, we are to understand—a king in the land of Shinar. To this day, every king, every descendant, every generation made in Nimrod's image wants what Nimrod wanted: power over others. Nimrod positioned himself where no man should ever be, in the place of God, and thus he believed the lives of others were his own. Nimrod's is the spirit of tyranny.

When power runs perpendicular to power, the inevitable collision will be directly proportional to the force, speed, magnitude, and mass involved. A backyard brawl over burgers may end in a shooting, but it will not end in mass destruction. When nation rises up against nation, the resulting explosion, especially in the twenty-first century, can mean global annihilation.

Now, consider that there are forces involved in these matters beyond the natural, forces that are supernatural. Power in the natural realm is a mystery that cannot be fully explained in earthly terms alone. In every human conflict there's a sense that something else, something beyond space and time, is involved. We have this sense because it is true. When the demented mind of some maniacal despot plots genocidal murder, there is a mind behind his mind. Every time a gang member puts his hand around the butt of a gun, there is a hand behind his hand.

This is the way of things in human history. The mystery of worldly power is its otherworldliness. Behind a raging king of monstrous evil and narcissistic self-worship is a dark, compelling spirit. The mind behind the mind is also the rage behind the rage. And so it goes.

In the plain of Shinar, in the land of Nimrod, a king erects a statue to himself and commands that it be worshipped. Deep within himself he knows he is not really a god. He cannot work miracles. He is not eternal. He knows this. The bowing of the multitudes is not really about worship in any true sense of worship, nor does the king really want to be prayed to. He wants to be bowed to, submitted to, surrendered to. It is all about power.

Three young men, enslaved captives, will not bow to an idol. Facing the threat of being incinerated alive, they still refuse to worship the statue. The contest is on. Now it's power against power. Yet this moment is not really about whether they bow and worship. Not exactly. Like frisky little Toto in *The Wizard of Oz*, let's snatch back the curtain to reveal what is really going on.

The real contest is the power behind the king's throne versus the throne of power behind the three young men. It is a tale of power against power, kingdom against kingdom. It is a drama in the supernatural realm played out in the natural realm. It's not just king versus slaves. It is seen versus unseen—the apparent conflict versus the invisible war. This is the truth of human history. The visible realm is ever colliding with the invisible realm, ever determined and shaped and even conquered by what is unseen.

When Moses confronted Pharaoh, when Elijah called out Ahab, and when John the Baptist denounced Herod, there were forces at work greater than the men themselves. Some prophets knew this and, in that knowledge, stood unbowed and unbeatable. Those kings who denied the prophetic utterances and acknowledged no power but their own were doomed.

Sometimes—though not often, because royal pride is a powerful obstacle—the tangential vectors of these prophet-versus-king inter-actions suddenly, dramatically realigned and shifted from a collision course onto a plane of agreement. The prophets who came

Read the story:

Daniel 3.

before kings as confronters became advisers, sometimes even valued counselors. Occasionally, the two adversaries became allies. This was never because the prophet backed down. Once the message of divine confrontation was delivered, no prophet, except Balaam, changed his tune. Of course, the most notable kingly reversal was David's in the matter of Bathsheba. The prophet Nathan's public denunciation of his king could have easily led to the death of one or both men, had David reacted as Herod did to John the Baptist. David's confession was not just the fruit of a guilty conscience. It was the submission of a king to a far greater sovereign, a repentant soul acknowledging the greater will of his God.

What could have easily escalated into an explosion of royal rage and the murder of a man of God was diffused by yielded confession. Conviction, brokenness, and repentance saved David's throne—and probably Nathan's life as well. What it came down to was this: David, who held all apparent human power, saw that he actually had none. A prophet, without any secular position and certainly not the empirical power that was David's, held the true reins of power. David discovered the secret contradiction that lies at the heart of the clash of kings and prophets. David won because he yielded to the higher power of the living God.

It does not always end this well. Herod murdered John the Baptist, decapitating him on the whim of a vengeful seductress. Herod and John are a study in contrast. Herod both hated and feared John the Baptist. John hated only sin and feared no king in this world. Herod had the power of Rome behind him. John had the power of heaven behind him. Herod's home was a palace. John's was a desert. To the human eye, it was John who lost his head and Herod who kept both his woman and his throne. However, in the all-important supernatural realm, it was John who gained a crown of glory and Herod who lost his soul. King Herod endured the wrath of almighty God and earned the eternal scorn of history. John endured the hatred of an incestuous puppet king but earned the embrace of the King of kings and the Lord of lords.

What follows in these pages are stories of prophets and the kings to whom they were sent by God. Written in blood and pain, these accounts are recorded in the Scriptures for our benefit. Lessons can be learned from every interaction of these ancient tyrant kings and the God-sent prophets with whom they went toe to toe. Their struggle is not theirs alone, nor were the higher truths of their experience for their time alone. They are for today, as they have been for all ages before. They are part of the ongoing warfare between the here and now and the not yet and forever.

It is kingdom against kingdom, power against power, the temporal against the eternal, the seen against the unseen. These, then, are tales of power, stories of what may be learned in the collision *of kings and prophets.*

Two great questions remain. Who are the real kings and who are the real prophets? The greater of these two questions is the latter. Phony kings are not nearly as dangerous as false prophets.

In 1869, in the tiny, impoverished village of Pokrovskoye, Siberia, a boy named Grigori Rasputin was born. In the manner of his people, he grew up an ignorant, illiterate peasant. Still, he seemed to have a gift. He impressed others with his "mystical powers," the power to heal, in particular. On the strength of these gifts, he moved to Saint Petersburg, where he was introduced to the royal family. Czarina Alexandra had heard of Rasputin's miracles and was drawn to the mystic because her son suffered from hemophilia. She believed having this man of spiritual power in the royal palace could keep her son from hemorrhaging to death, and it seemed, for a time, that it might be true. On several occasions, Rasputin had prayed for the little boy and the bleeding stopped. The rough mystic thus became a fixture in Russia's royal household.

Rasputin may have had supernatural powers, but he was not a moral man. He was well known for his drunkenness and extramarital affairs, and some claim he took bribes and extorted sexual favors from people wanting access to the czar. His behavior became infamous. All of Russia knew of his lasciviousness, but Alexandra would not send the man away. She feared too desperately for the life of her son. Sensing the tide shifting against him, Rasputin publicly and dramatically declared that Russia would lose World War I unless the czar himself went to the front and commanded the troops. The czar, a man easily duped, obeyed the manipulative prophecy. This, of course, removed the czar from the palace and gave Rasputin unhindered access to the czarina.

The situation became so desperate that finally a band of Russian nobles murdered Rasputin on December 30, 1916. Grigori Rasputin has become synonymous with false prophets and dark, sinister mystics who exerted undue influence on kings, emperors, and generals throughout history.

On May 26, 1785, General George Washington, who was soon to be elected president of the United States, wrote in his diary for that day: "Upon my return found Mr. Magowan, and a Doctr. Coke & a Mr. Asbury here—the two last Methodest Preachers recommended by Genl. Roberdeau—the same who were expected yesterday....After Dinner Mr. Coke & Mr. Asbury went away."[6] That's all the general wrote of this meeting.

Yet on that same day, Dr. Coke, a Welsh missionary sent to America by John Wesley to help Francis Asbury administer the burgeoning Methodist Church in the New World, wrote in his diary that he and Asbury had pled with General Washington to sign a petition opposing slavery and to free his own slaves. The men made it clear that they believed the future of the United States was in the balance. Washington expressed his opposition to slavery personally, but he declined to sign the petition or to free his slaves.[7]

General Washington provided in his will that the 123 slaves he owned would be freed at his wife, Martha's, death. He wanted to make sure his beloved wife was cared for. Yet the year the general died, Martha—a devoutly Christian, compassionate woman—freed the family's slaves.

The visit between Francis Asbury and George Washington happened in 1785. Some eighty years later, in 1865, the Thirteenth Amendment was passed, freeing the slaves but only after the nation had been torn to shreds and more than seven hundred thousand Americans had been killed in combat.

Life and history are filled with what-ifs. What if the emperor had seen Rasputin for the evil fraud that he was? What difference would it have made? Would the Romanov family still have been executed by communists? Would Russia be what it is today? We cannot know.

A greater and more poignant what-if: What if General Washington had signed that petition in 1785? What if he had freed his slaves and then convinced Jefferson to do the same? Indeed, what if he and all the other slave owners who were at the Constitutional Convention had together taken a bold stand to outlaw slavery from the beginning of the republic? Maybe seven hundred thousand Americans wouldn't have died in the nightmare of the Civil War. Again, we will never know.

The Bible is filled with stories of leaders, kings, and generals whose lives and nations were impacted by the spiritual or prophetic counsel they either received or rejected. In this book I want to explore the interactions between these kings and prophets. These interactions are about the natural transformed by the supernatural, and of the earthly, daily, and almost mundane intersected by an anointed spokesman for the will of God. What is there to learn from these intersections?

We should start by asking this: Who were the prophets? They were people who, first of all, were called into the office of prophet by God. Some were called in truly supernatural encounters, miraculous moments of divine experience, like Moses at the burning bush or Isaiah in the famous heavenly throne room. In that account of his call, Isaiah describes an astonishingly extravagant vision of the resplendent glory of God.

> In the year that King Uzziah died, I saw the Lord, high and exalted, seated on a throne; and the train of his robe filled the temple. Above him were seraphim, each with six wings: With two wings they covered their faces, with two they covered their feet, and with two they were flying. And they were calling to one another:
>
> > "Holy, holy, holy is the LORD Almighty;
> > the whole earth is full of his glory."
>
> At the sound of their voices the doorposts and thresholds shook and the temple was filled with smoke.
> "Woe to me!" I cried. "I am ruined! For I am a man of unclean lips, and I live among a people of unclean lips, and my eyes have seen the King, the LORD Almighty."
> Then one of the seraphim flew to me with a live coal in his hand, which he had taken with tongs from the altar. With it he touched my mouth and said, "See,

this has touched your lips; your guilt is taken away and your sin atoned for."

Then I heard the voice of the Lord saying, "Whom shall I send? And who will go for us?"

And I said, "Here am I. Send me!"[8]

Isaiah's experience is just the kind of transforming supernatural encounter through which some of the prophets were called. For others, there was no dramatic moment, no singular supernatural experience. It was more than a one-time event. Sometimes the "call" experience was a lifetime of hearing the inner voice of God.

One of the greatest examples of this is Samuel. In his first book, the prophet describes his visit to the house of Jesse in Bethlehem. He is there to anoint the new king of Israel. It is a moment filled with import. History hangs in the balance. Jesse is told to bring his sons to stand before the prophet. Samuel is willing to anoint any of the young men with oil to signify who is to become the next king of Israel, thus succeeding Saul. Yet God forbids him to anoint any of them. With what was surely a sense of frustration, Samuel asks Jesse one of the funniest questions in the whole Bible: "Are these all the sons you have?"[9] As if Jesse might not be sure!

Jesse's answer is also humorous. It is a perfect example of how God works through the exceptional and unexpected. Jesse says, in essence, "Well, OK, there is one other son, but he's kind of a weird little kid." Samuel immediately senses something from God. He says, "Send for him; we will not sit down until he arrives." Finally, they bring David in. The Lord speaks to Samuel, "Rise and anoint him; this is the one."[10] Samuel quickly anoints the boy, but there is no burning bush. There is no open vision of the heavenly throne room. No, David is anointed king of Israel because a disciplined prophet knows how, despite what he sees, to hear the voice of God because he has been hearing it for a lifetime.

First, prophets hear from God. Secondly, they speak for God. Sometimes they call people, nations, or cities to repentance or they summon them to align with God's will. Sometimes they confront society itself for neglecting God's law. Throughout Israel's history, prophets were often called upon to confront the almost ever-present sin of idolatry. Many of the prophets, especially those who wrote their messages to the people of God, were deeply concerned about social justice, the corruption of the law, the exploitation of the poor, and the ever-pressing sin of sexual immorality.

Prophets were also told to confront great leaders because those leaders represented the nation as a whole. This was particularly true of King David. It can be said that as it was with David, so it was with the nation. At other times prophets confronted leaders for their own personal sin, about matters in their individual lives. Nathan's denunciation of David for his sin with Bathsheba is an example. So is John the Baptist's denunciation of Herod for an incestuous relationship with his brother's wife.

This task of confronting and challenging the powerful informs most people's image of prophets. We often think of them as dark and forbidding, angry men filled with the wrath of God who fiercely confronted sin and wickedness. There is certainly this aspect of prophetic ministry in Scripture. Yet at times the prophet does not appear to rebuke but rather counsel or even comfort. This was the manner in which Francis Asbury spoke to George Washington about slavery. It is also the spirit in which many a biblical prophet spoke to kings and generals. They were sent to provide supernatural assistance. They were sent to announce impending miracles and the care of God for those faithful to Him.

Finally, we should know that the prophets themselves were not flawless human beings. The idea that prophets were perfect ignores the basic reality that they were people. The truth is that they were human beings who carried their humanity with them into the office of prophet. Sometimes that humanity really showed itself.

The prophet Jonah was extremely guilty of a vile sort of bigotry. He did not want God to save the pagans in Nineveh. In fact, he wanted God to kill them all. When the Lord sent Jonah to Nineveh to call the city to repentance, Jonah sulked and rebelled. We are told that Jonah was furious with God. He even admitted to being so angry he could die. The man was riddled with self-pity, self-will, and prejudice.

Elijah was certainly not perfect. Though he was one of the greatest of all the prophets, he struggled with depression, rejection, and a bit of a persecution complex. In fact, Elijah, the great man of God, also battled a shocking, debilitating fear. He often experienced tremendous supernatural victories, and then, nearly with the next breath, he retreated in terror of the very person he had just miraculously defeated.

There is also the mystifying example of Miriam, who is listed as one of the prophets. We are told in Scripture that she was filled with both envy for her own brother and racial prejudice. She rebelled against Moses, in part because his wife was not a Hebrew. She helped lead a mutiny against not only her own brother but against God's anointed vessel for the deliverance of Israel. She was a mutineer. So was Aaron, who is also called a prophet. Though he was anointed as a priest of God, we learn that he made a golden calf for the people to worship.

We find such aberrations in the lives of prophets again and again in Scripture. Even Abram is an example of this. Though he is called a prophet in the Bible, he shows a stunning level of cowardice and duplicity. Here is one of the great lessons to be gained through all of this: the calling of God does not erase the humanity of the prophet but uses it. Thus, the sinful man and the anointed man are operating side by side in the same body. This encourages me immensely.

This book is largely about how divine counsel was expressed through flawed prophets to even more flawed leaders. At the end of this book I hope you will understand much more about God's dealings with humankind. More than that I hope you will be encouraged about how God can use even the likes of you and me. We know we are flawed. We know we have fallen short. Yet we also yearn to take hold of that for which Christ Jesus has taken hold of us.

Before we begin, I should tell you how I chose which prophets to write about and a bit about the number of prophets in Scripture. As a guide, I used the work of the French, eleventh-century rabbi known as Rashi. That's not his name; it's an acronym used to honor him. Rabbi Shlomo Yitzḥaqi was so revered for his clear and lucid writing about the Talmud that his followers used certain letters from his name. This is how he is known to history.[11]

Rashi formulated a list of who the Jews consider to be the prophets of Israel.[12] I'm going to work from Rashi's list, but I'm also including two important figures from the New Testament. According to this Jewish understanding, there are forty-six male prophets and seven female prophets. I won't list all forty-six, but the seven females are Sarah (Sarai), Miriam, Deborah, Hannah, Abigail, Huldah, and Esther (Hadassah). This list of female prophets reveals much about God's willingness to use women in His work. That, however, is for yet another book.

In Hebrew the word for *prophet* is simply *nebi*. When the word is plural, as in "the prophets," it is *nebim*. Literally translated, the word means "spokesman." I have spent a great deal of time in West Africa, where I gained insight into the meaning of the word *spokesman*. Because a chief traditionally considered it beneath him to speak directly to people, he had a spokesman do it for him. The spokesman carried a tall staff topped with an ornate decoration, such as a lion. All who saw the bearer of the staff knew he spoke for a chief.

I have seen this many times. The process was fascinating to watch. Someone would approach to make a petition. The chief's spokesman would listen. Then the spokesman would approach the throne. He and the chief would whisper back and forth for quite some time. Then the spokesman would return to his position before the petitioner, pound his staff on the ground, and loudly issue the chief's verdict.

This is a clear picture of the role of a prophet, particularly in the Hebrew understanding. The prophet enters God's presence, hears His will, and then proclaims it to the people. Just as with the West African chiefs, there is no confusion between the spokesman and the chief. Should a spokesman claim to be chief, he would be killed. The chief speaks. He speaks through his spokesman. The spokesman knows his limited, defined role. So it was in West Africa. So it was in Scripture.

Obviously, I have not included all the prophets in Rashi's list. I've made selections, and I want you to know why. I want to deal with the intersection, the clash, between these prophets and their contemporary kings. Sometimes there is a head-to-head confrontation. Sometimes there is a gentler interaction involving welcomed advice and counsel. Yet there is always an intersection of the human with the divine. These interactions had inevitable friction. Prophets are about the heavenly kingdom. Kings are about their earthly kingdom, the natural kingdom. Prophets are about the throne of God. Kings are about earthly thrones and power. There is drama here. There is contention. Yet there is also wisdom and understanding for our own time and our own lives.

CHAPTER 2

Abraham: The First Prophet?

Now return the man's wife, for he is a prophet, and he will pray for you and you will live. But if you do not return her, you may be sure that you and all who belong to you will die.

—Genesis 20:7

ABRAHAM MAY SEEM an odd choice for the opening subject of a book about kings and prophets since many would say he was neither. It is likely that most contemporary Christians have never thought of Abraham as a prophet, yet the Bible clearly states that he was. In Genesis, God spoke to King Abimelech, the unfortunate man who had taken Abraham's wife as his own. God comforted Abimelech in a dream because he had erred "with a clear conscience" but told him he should "now return the man's wife, for *he is a prophet*, and he will pray for you and you will live."[1]

Since God Himself called Abraham a prophet, who are we to argue?

Yet given all I've said about the value of looking at the interaction of prophets and kings, the next question has to be whether we see prophet Abraham interacting with kings. Again, the unlikely answer is an emphatic yes! Actually, Abraham interacts with a full dozen kings—nine of them in one battle alone. This happens when Chedorlaomer, an Elamite king, and his three allies attack the king of Sodom along with the king of Gomorrah and three of their allies.[2] That's nine kings in one battle. Abraham also has dealings with Pharaoh regarding his wife, who was his half-sister, and he has that other embarrassing moment regarding Abimelech and his wife. Finally, he has dealings with the mysterious King Melchizedek. This makes twelve kings in all. Clearly, we have full biblical authorization to say that Abraham is a prophet and he repeatedly dealt with kings. During this part of Abraham's life, he was still named Abram, so I will refer to him as such. Much later God changed his name to Abraham.

Abram's conflict with kings began with his troublesome nephew Lot. You may recall that God had so blessed Abram and Lot that as they made their way from Ur of Chaldees into the Promised Land, their herds became too large to travel together and share the same pastures. There was tension between their herdsmen and shepherds. So Abram went to Lot and said, in essence, "Look, let's just divide things up. We're still kinsmen, we're going to be kinsmen, but there's no use for us to have conflict. You choose anywhere you want to go. If you go south, I'll go north. If you go north, I'll go south."

—————— ❧ ——————

Read the story:

Genesis 13.

—————— ❦ ——————

The Bible tells us that Lot lifted up his eyes and looked toward Sodom. He saw that the plain was well watered everywhere and that there were great cities. So Lot went in that direction. At this point in the story, we read a telling verse, "Lot...pitched his tents near Sodom."[3] In other words, he attached his sense of identity and prosperity to the prevailing city of Sodom. Of course, we learn that over time this move compromised him and ultimately destroyed him.

—————— ❧ ——————

Read the story:

Genesis 18–19.

—————— ❦ ——————

Indeed, the wickedness of Sodom and Gomorrah became so horrible that God sent angels to destroy those two cities. Before they did, the angels visited Abram and told him what they were about to do. This initiates one of the great negotiations in history. Abram tries to make a deal. He says to the Lord, "OK, if there are fifty righteous people, You're not going to destroy the city, right?" And the Lord responds, "No, for fifty I won't." Abram then says, "OK, but what about forty-five?" And so it goes until, finally, Abram and the Lord agree that if there are ten righteous men, the Lord won't destroy the cities.

What follows is hard to watch. The angels arrive in Lot's city. There is a ghoulish scene in which a sex-crazed crowd wants to have sex with the holy beings. Lot feels it necessary to offer his virgin daughters to appease them.

The angels have seen enough. They strike the crowd with blindness and tell Lot to get his family together and leave because they are going to destroy this wicked society. Lot warns his sons-in-law, but they don't take him seriously. Lot then tries to escape with his wife and daughters, but his wife disobeys the angels' command not to look back and becomes a pillar of salt.

This is important. Jesus said it a different way in the New Testament: "No one who puts a hand to the plow and looks back is fit for service in the kingdom of God."[4] In other words, Lot's wife looks back fondly at all that she was losing in Sodom. She's not thinking about the wickedness, she's not thinking about the judgment of God. She's thinking about the women in her bridge club. She's talking about the girls at the country club. She was happy and rich and well thought of. Lot had become a judge in Sodom, we are told. So as she is forced to leave, she looks back longingly at the sinful ways she has been commanded to abandon. And she dies.

Every moment of this and what follows is pregnant with

meaning. The angels try to send Lot to the mountains. He pleads and asks them to send him to a little town called Zoar. He's too afraid. He's too weak. Finally, the angels relent and send Lot to Zoar. We are supposed to know that Zoar means "small" in Hebrew.[5] It's an indicator of how far Lot has fallen. However, even Zoar is not enough. Lot allows fear to drive him to a cave outside of Zoar. It is there that he gets drunk, impregnates both of his daughters, and ends up fathering the two tribes that will bedevil his descendants for generations to come, the Ammonites and the Moabites.

It all started with a choice of direction. Lot pitched his tents toward Sodom, and the direction he chose sealed his fate.

When I was in college, I got a job as the head counselor of a day camp. We held camp during each day of the week, but on Friday we would camp out overnight. We did this on several hundred acres on which we were free to choose our own site each time. One Friday night we got a late start. We ended up pitching our tents in the semidarkness and, frankly, we weren't quite sure where we were.

Since I was twenty-one and was leading a bunch of fifth-grade boys, I naturally felt it necessary to tell them a ghost story while we gobbled s'mores around the campfire. I did my job well and scared the liver out of those boys. I had them pretty primed. At midnight we heard the most horrible, eerie sound. It sounded like banshees had descended on us. I sat bolt upright in my sleeping bag, and within seconds those boys dove into my tent like they were diving into a foxhole under a barrage. They were crying and screaming, and I realized that the only way to settle them down was to bravely leave the tent and promptly surrender to whatever horrible creature was howling.

I got my flashlight and went outside. When I did, I saw that we had set up our tents by a fence, and just on the other side was a huge, long-eared mule. I'm not talking about a sweet little burro like you see in television advertising. I am talking about a mean old army mule. It was braying and carrying on like he was announcing the end of the world, or perhaps causing it.

Here is the lesson: be careful where you pitch your tent because there may be a jackass on the other side of the fence.

I want to focus, however, on an episode that occurs while Lot is still at Sodom, before the great destruction. Sodom and Gomorrah, along with three other small cities, have been paying tribute to the Elamite king for twelve years. This means that five kings—really, they were glorified mayors, tribal chieftains, or warlords who had

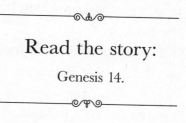

Read the story:

Genesis 14.

little private armies to protect themselves—had been required to pay tribute to the greater Elamite king. (Elam, by the way, is in the southern part of modern-day Iran, pre-Iranian Persia, on the Persian Gulf opposite the Arabian Peninsula.) After a dozen years the five kings decide that they are finally strong enough to refuse to pay tribute to the king of Elam any longer.

The predictable happens. The Elamite king, along

with three of his allies, marches against the five kings—including the kings of Sodom and Gomorrah, rulers of the regions where Lot lives. The Elamites burn the towns, loot everything they can, confiscate all the cities' treasure, and take many captives. Lot and his family are among them.

While the Elamites march their captives back to Persia, a man who escaped the devastation makes his way to Abram to tell him what has happened. Abram is urged to rescue Lot, and he doesn't need to be persuaded. He immediately rouses his private army of 318 soldiers and leads them as they ride through the night to intercept the Elamite forces.

When he comes upon the Elamite camp, presumably Abram finds the foreign army celebrating its victory. Perhaps the soldiers are drunk, and there is great carousing and boasting and enjoying the spoils of war as victorious armies tend to do. At any rate Abram's little army attacked in the night, killing many and pursuing the rest all the way into Syria, rescuing Lot, his family, and the other people in the process.

The king of Sodom had somehow escaped being taken captive by the Elamites. When Abram returned from his victory, this king went out to meet him. He said to Abram, "You can take all the loot, take all that the Elamites stole, just give me the people and we'll go back to Sodom." Abram's answer is revealing. Let's read it in full:

> With raised hand I have sworn an oath to the LORD, God Most High, Creator of heaven and earth, that I will accept nothing belonging to you, not even a thread or the strap of a sandal, so that you will never be able to say, "I made Abram rich." I will accept nothing but what my men have eaten and the share

that belongs to the men who went with me—to Aner, Eshkol and Mamre. Let them have their share.[6]

There is an important lesson in this. We see it in Abram's posture toward the king of Sodom. Abram tells us by example that there are some kings that you just stay away from. Lot's compromise, his accommodation, his participation in wrongdoing, his profit from Sodom all earned him and his family complete destruction. It started with the choice of direction he made. Lot pitched his tent toward Sodom because it was like Egypt, but Egypt is a place of captivity. Abram said, "I am pitching my tent toward God and His Promised Land." Abram says there are some kings you just avoid, and some directions you don't take when you are pursuing the purposes of God.

We don't often think of prophets as warriors, but it is not altogether unusual for prophets to go to war throughout the Old Testament. Remember that when Saul did not kill Agag the king of the Amalekites as he should have, Samuel the prophet found the man and did the deed himself. The King James Bible records the moment this way: "And Samuel hewed Agag in pieces before the LORD in Gilgal."[7] Remember also that when Elijah was confronting the prophets of Baal, he called for the death of 450 false prophets of Baal and 400 prophets of Asherah.[8] This meant the death of 850 men in one afternoon. This helps us understand that at least some of the prophets in the Bible are best understood as "warrior prophets." This is how we should see Abram in this story.

Certainly, this great warrior prophet teaches us, first, that there are some kings you should avoid entirely. But there are other kings, strongholds, and powers that you have to fight. You have to go on the offensive. This is a perfect picture of our offensive weaponry against the armies of darkness. We don't have to hide and cower from the forces of darkness that come against us to try to corrupt or steal what is ours. We can fight; we should fight. The weapons of our warfare are mighty. The apostle Paul refers to offensive weapons in his description of the weapons of our warfare.[9] This tells us there are times we have to attack, times we have to stand up to Satan and fight him.

There are two equal and opposite lessons in this story. Abram embodies both. Some kings are simply to be avoided. Stay clear of Sodom. It's that simple. Others you must attack. You must go on the offensive. Abram also presents a clear picture of how we are to care for lost people and those in bondage. Our ability to perform spiritual warfare and to function in it springs from our absolute confidence in the victory of God. If we live with an equal fear of Satan and an equal fear of God, then we will never be able to do spiritual warfare. We must go after those in the captivity of evil forces, confident in our faith.

A story is told of Martin Luther, the father of the Protestant movement. It seems he was awakened from sleep one night because he heard a noise. He lit a candle, looked around his room, and saw Satan standing between where he lay in his bed and the only way of escape. Luther is supposed to have said, "Oh, it's just you. I was afraid it was a burglar." And he blew out the candle and went back to sleep.

This is the prophet's stance against the kings of evil who come to attack and steal, kidnap and destroy. We don't have to cower in the darkness. We attack. We attack all night if we have to. We catch the Elamites asleep. We destroy them. We have no fear. We do not have to sit passively by and let Satan kidnap our loved ones. Some kings you simply steer away from. Some kings you have to fight.

When Abram returns from his shocking victory, the king of Sodom is there to greet him, ready to make a generous proposal, which he subsequently did. However, before he could say a word, a mysterious king named Melchizedek steps up. His appearance is in a truly intriguing passage of scripture. Melchizedek actually interrupts Abram's interaction with the king of Sodom.

In the middle of Abram's interaction with the king of Sodom, Melchizedek, who is called the king of Salem, draws Abram aside. Let's look at this episode in full as it appears in Scripture.

> Then Melchizedek king of Salem brought out bread and wine. He was priest of God Most High, and he blessed Abram, saying, "Blessed be Abram by God Most High, Creator of heaven and earth. And praise be to God Most High, who delivered your enemies into your hand." Then Abram gave him a tenth of everything.[10]

Melchizedek serves Abram bread and wine. Does that sound familiar? This is particularly significant since Melchizedek is called a priest as well as a king. Then Abram tithes to Melchizedek. We Christians don't have any problem with the idea of Abram tithing to a man who is a "priest of God Most High." But in rabbinical writings through the centuries, there's a great deal of controversy and debate about who tithes to whom in this story. You see, in Hebrew the pronouns used here are interchangeable. It reads simply, "He tithed to him." That's all Hebrew scholars have to go on. We Christians, of course, have the reference to this story in the New Testament Book of Hebrews, which tells us specifically that "Abram gave him a tenth of everything."[11] Not having the Book of Hebrews, though, the rabbis have fought for hundreds and hundreds of years over who is tithing to whom. Frankly, it makes more sense that Abram would tithe to Melchizedek. Why would Melchizedek tithe to Abram, a man he had just met and who had no priestly role? So we take the story as it is. Abram is served bread and wine—communion! He then tithes to this mysterious priest called Melchizedek. Of course, this interaction is a prefiguring of Jesus' high priestly role, as we learn in Hebrews 7, but that is far beyond our purpose here.

What is more germane to the point of this book is what happens when Abram turns back to the king of Sodom, who is prepared to make Abram an offer: "You take all the loot you gained from defeating the foreign kings. Just give me the people."

Abram refuses. He turns to the king of Sodom and says, "You take everything. I don't want anything." It is interesting that he uses a unique parallelism in Hebrew. It means, in an idiomatic way familiar at the time, "from one extreme to another." In other words, "I don't want anything, from start to finish, from beginning to end, from one side to the other."

We should remember why Abram said this. He had taken

a vow, with raised hand, before "the Lᴏʀᴅ, God Most High, Creator of heaven and earth." He would accept nothing belonging to the king of Sodom, not even a thread or a shoelace. No one, certainly not the king of Sodom—that famously immoral place—would ever be able to say that they had made Abram rich. Such was Abram's devotion; such was his character.

Some kings you simply must avoid. We can imagine that the king of Sodom had probably drawn Lot into his inner circle, into his clutches. He had made deals with Abram's nephew and entangled him in the culture of Sodom. The man probably thought he could do the same to Abram. He couldn't, and this may be part of the reason for the story of Melchizedek appearing where it does. Before the king of Sodom can make an offer that likely has strings attached, Melchizedek steps in. He serves Abram what we Christians understand to be communion. Abram tithes to him, which indicates that Abram was honoring God with his wealth, acknowledging God as the provider of all Abram had.

It isn't surprising, then, that immediately after this Abram turns to the king of Sodom and says, "I don't want anything you've got." Clearly, Abram knew the character of the man and knew the vile place he ruled over. He wanted nothing to do with any of it, particularly having just per-haps been newly sanctified by the ministry of Melchizedek and by making an offering through a priest of God. In a freshly holy state, Abram wanted nothing at all to do with wickedness.

Notice also that Abram does not hold the other people who fought with him to his level of ethics. He had brought his own soldiers to the recent fight, 318 in all, as well as other local clans. While he wouldn't take any of the loot, Abram says, "Let them have whatever they want." In other words, he didn't expect them to live by his ethical decisions. He just made his decisions known, certain that they were the right thing for him. It was as though he were saying, "This is where I am." There is power in this, and there is also power in avoiding the legalism of insisting that others measure up to your ethical commitments.

The ultimate lesson in all this, though, is a simple truth: there is only one King worthy of worship. This understanding comes to us by knowing who Melchizedek is. He is mentioned in the Bible in only three places: Genesis, Psalms, and Hebrews. So why is pondering his story worth our while? Because our Lord Jesus Christ is called a High Priest after the order of Melchizedek. This changes everything—and is it ever thrilling!

Now, there is an interesting distinction between Western Christian, particularly American, reasoning on the one hand and traditional Jewish reasoning on the other. For Americans especially, what is really important is what you know. What are the facts? What information are you given? Knowledge is king to us in the West, and it's emphasized in nearly every endeavor of life, especially in interpreting Scripture. Yet in Jewish thinking, the emphasis is often on what you don't know. In other words, the greater truth is revealed in the information you don't have.

This is truly relevant when we come to Melchizedek. Notice that we don't know anything about his birth, his family, or his upbringing. This is maddening, to the Jewish way of thinking in particular. Hebrew scripture focuses constantly on genealogy, origins, and family lines. Who your people are and where you come from is vital to knowing who you are in the Hebrew mindset. Yet hardly any of these normally important questions are answered when it comes to Melchizedek. He just appears.

Yet the New Testament Book of Hebrews, which was written to Jews, builds upon this lack of information about Melchizedek. It acknowledges that we know nothing about this man's background, that he seems to have no beginning, and that his death is not recorded, so in essence, he has no end. Rather than try to solve these mysteries, the Book of Hebrews simply makes a comparison: Jesus is our High Priest after the order of Melchizedek.

Let's take a close look at what the author of the Book of Hebrews has to say. Having simply stated in the last sentence of Hebrews 6 that Jesus is a High Priest in the order of Melchizedek, the author begins Hebrews 7 by going deeper into the meaning of Melchizedek.

> This Melchizedek was king of Salem and priest of God Most High. He met Abraham returning from the defeat of the kings and blessed him, and Abraham gave him a tenth of everything. First, the name Melchizedek means "king of righteousness"; then also, "king of Salem" means "king of peace." Without father or mother, without genealogy, without beginning of days or end of life, resembling the Son of God, he remains a priest forever.[12]

The author of Hebrews continues like this for another dozen verses, exploring what may be known of Melchizedek and how great he was. Finally, he makes the all-important application to Jesus.

> And what we have said is even more clear if another priest like Melchizedek appears, one who has become a priest not on the basis of a regulation as to his ancestry but on the basis of the power of an indestructible life. For it is declared: "You are a priest forever, in the order of Melchizedek."[13]

One school of thought is that Melchizedek was actually Jesus making an Old Testament personal appearance. Others see Melchizedek as a prefigurement of Christ, not Christ Himself but an Old Testament revelation of Christ. In this thinking Melchizedek is an Old Testament archetype of Jesus. The Bible doesn't actually say that Jesus is Melchizedek. It says that Jesus is our High Priest in the order of Melchizedek, after the kind of Melchizedek.

However, let's not get bogged down in the debate that surrounds Jesus and Melchizedek. Let's learn the lesson God wants us to learn from this story. Picture the moment. Abram is returning from battle. He's tired, as are his men. They've ridden and fought all night. They are caked in blood and have the clash of battle still ringing in their ears. At this vulnerable moment, the king of Sodom steps up to Abram and says, "Take all the money you want." Destinies are in the balance at this moment. Covenants are being tested. Character is being exposed. Then God steps in. Right in the middle of the interaction between Abram and the king of Sodom, Melchizedek appears to intervene. "Wait a minute. Listen to me before you act. Sit down here for a moment. Commune with me. Have some bread, some wine. Reflect for a moment with God's representation standing near, the space surrounding you filled with the Spirit of God." Rising from this beautiful moment, Abram turns to the king of Sodom and says, "I don't want anything you've got."

There's a change, a different feel from before. A different spirit pervades. All because Melchizedek, the king of peace, has stepped in.

Melchizedek's appearance notwithstanding, Abram is heroic here. He takes a noble stand and does so at a moment that might have meant disaster for him. Abram was not always such a stalwart, sterling example of virtue. Let's remember a bit of the past so that this moment before Melchizedek has even greater meaning.

Remember that Abram twice surrendered his wife to other men out of fear for himself. This may be hard for us to imagine, but it is true. He did it once in Egypt when he told Pharaoh that Sarai, who became Sarah, was his sister. This was half true because Abram and Sarai were half-siblings. So fearing what might befall him, he tells

Read the story:

Genesis 12:10–20; 20:1–18.

Sarai to tell everyone that she is his sister. Pharaoh—smitten with the stunning Sarai—gives Abram a huge amount of money and takes Abram's wife into his harem.

Thankfully, Pharaoh doesn't sleep with Sarai. This is consistent with what we know of harems. It was not unusual for a woman to go into a harem for a long time of preparation and training before she appeared before the king or ruler. It wasn't the custom for a woman to go into a harem and straight to Pharaoh's bed. There was always a season of training and beautification. We see this, for example, in the story of Esther.

Despite this, diseases come upon the land. Pharaoh isn't stupid. He realizes this must be a judgment somehow connected to this new woman. He says to Abram, "You told me she was your sister. I'm innocent. You're the one who's guilty. Why did you do this?" Fearing more judgment, Pharaoh gives Abram great wealth and sends him and Sarai on their way. Frankly, the Egyptians can't wait for these newcomers to leave!

Now, we would all like to believe that Abram rode along on his camel thinking, "Man, that was stupid and cowardly. What in the world was I thinking? I'll never do that again. I sinned once. I learned my lesson. I'll never sin that way again." But he did. Exactly that way.

How very like us Abram was. After deceiving Pharaoh, he heads down the road and enters the region of the Philistines. There he encounters a great king named Abimelech. Once again moved by fear, Abram tells Sarai to tell everyone that she is his sister. Once again, the great patriarch surrenders his wife out of fear for his own well-being. Naturally, Abimelech takes the beautiful Sarai as his own. Notice that he just took her. He does not pay a bride price or negotiate with Abram. He just takes Sarai.

And God intervenes. He speaks to Abimelech in a dream and tells him, "You are as good as dead because of the woman you have taken; she is a married woman."[14] Abimelech, of course, protests. He says, "I'm innocent. He told me she was his sister." And God says, "I know, I know, so I'm going to let you get out of this. Send him away; he's a prophet."

We see something of Abram's early character in these stories, don't we? He could be cowardly. He could let fear dominate him. It is unsettling to see our sins repeated by our children, and Abram's son Isaac did exactly the same thing out of exactly the same motivation. When Isaac and Rebekah go to live among the Philistines during a famine, they also have to deal with Abimelech. And sure enough, Isaac tells the Philistine king that Rebekah is his sister because he is afraid Abimelech's men might kill him, so beautiful is his wife.[15] The same actions in the same situation because of the same unresolved weakness. How horrible it is, how discouraging to see our sins in our sons.

Let me not end this chapter with a negative reflection on Abram but instead share a powerful image from this great man's life that prefigured much to come in history after Abram was gone.

First, we know that he was a great patriarch. He was the primal Hebrew. He was the father of Judaism. He has been revered throughout history for all these roles. Judaism claims him. Christianity claims him. Islam claims him. He is as much a father to humanity as any man who has ever lived.

Yet there is an episode in his life which not only confirms that he is a prophet—beyond the single verse we have already seen—but indicates how central to God's plan for the world Abram truly was.

Here is a summary of what Scripture tells us: God has

spoken to Abram and said that he should not be afraid, that God is his shield and his very great reward. Yet Abram is not comforted. He's concerned that he has no heir and that a foreigner who works for him will be his heir unless God acts. So God promises him again that his heirs will be as numerous as the stars and that he has been given the

Promised Land. Then God commands him to make a sacrifice.

Abram does as he is told. He splits the animals in half and lays the pieces

————— ❦ —————

Read the story:

Genesis 15.

————— ❦ —————

out. Then he waits. He drives off birds of prey that come to consume the sacrifice. He waits some more. And God begins to speak. Amazingly, He begins speaking of what is coming centuries in the future. Here is what He says:

> Know for certain that for four hundred years your descendants will be strangers in a country not their own and that they will be enslaved and mistreated there. But I will punish the nation they serve as slaves, and afterward they will come out with great possessions. You, however, will go to your ancestors in peace and be buried at a good old age. In the fourth generation your descendants will come back here, for the sin of the Amorites has not yet reached its full measure.[16]

Two amazing events follow. God reaffirms His promise to give Abram's descendants the Land, and He even describes its dimensions. Then this happens: "When the sun had set and darkness had fallen, a smoking firepot with a blazing torch appeared and passed between the pieces."[17]

To understand this, we need to know a bit about an ancient Hebrew practice. If two people were going to strike a covenant with each other, a sacrifice was made. Animals would be offered and laid open on the ground. Once this was done, a meaningful ritual followed.

The two people making covenant would link arms and walk among the sacrifices. Picture this in your mind as a figure eight. In other words, imagine the two covenant makers, arm in arm, walking the pattern of the number eight among the sacrificial animals. They would walk in the middle of the sacrifices.[18] This might be referred to as the "valley." Do the famous words come to mind? "Yea, though I walk through the valley of the shadow of death, I will fear no evil: for thou art with me."[19]

Then they would walk on the outside of the sacrifices. They would keep walking, keep stepping off that figure eight, keep weaving among the sacrifices. Soon they would return to the "valley" again, where the blood and the stench and the death were. Images of what evils might come in the future formed in their minds. This deepened their covenant, demonstrating what their bond would mean in looming days of trouble.

Here is what I want you to know. In this spectacular moment when that smoking firepot appeared with a blazing torch and passed among the pieces, that was God passing through the sacrifice alone. Certainly God was signifying He would be with Abram on the less challenging outer portions. Likewise He would be with Abram in the valley, in the gore and pain and fear. This is astonishing proof that God's covenant with Abram was God's work and God's alone. A one-sided covenant is a covenant of grace.

This was the core truth of Abram's life. He was a flawed man sometimes dominated by fear and given to cowardice. Yet he knew a covenantal God, a God who had committed to him and his people. This is what made Abram a patriarch. This is what made him the possessor of a Promised Land. This is what made him the founder of faith. And this is what made him a prophet of God.

LESSONS FROM OLD DR. MARK ABOUT ABRAHAM

Enjoy victory after the victory.

Remember this: After a battle, whether you win or lose, you need a fresh encounter with God. Immediately after his victory over the kings who had kidnapped Lot, but before he answered the king of Sodom, Abram communed with the priest of Salem. After duking it out with one "king" or another, even if you win, you will be more exhausted than you think. Tired folks make bad choices, and bad choices can snatch defeat from the jaws of victory. Let the High Priest of our faith restore what you lost in the fray. Fresh from His presence, you will make the next right choice.

Live and lead without fear.

Our covenant with God rests on the foundation of God's perfection, not ours. Abram was hardly perfect. He was a great man and a great prophet, but he was not perfect. We are not perfect, and our pretend perfection is a poor disguise. We occasionally fool ourselves, but only briefly, and we fool no one else at all. Nothing eternal rests on our carnal selves. All we believe in and hope for rest solely on the character of God. We can live and lead without fear, confident in life and death, because our covenant with God rests on the character of God.

Be careful where you pitch your tent.

Lot is a cautionary tale. Sodom looked inviting, prosperous, and, well, easier. Long before Lot was kidnapped from Sodom, he was kidnapped *by* Sodom. Compromise leads inexorably toward destruction. Sodom corrupted him, and his life ended in a cave where he impregnated his own daughters. Pitch your tent toward Sodom and receive Sodom's destruction. Pitch your tent in the center of God's will for your life and receive His blessings.

Know when to fight and when to flee.

Life is full of "kings." Some kings are threatening, such as an unreasonable boss or an overwrought customer. Some are seductive. Like Abram, we must discern which to fight and which to flee. Getting that right may mean the difference between doom and deliverance.

Some folks' default position is to fight. Their life is constant turmoil. Everything is a matter of principle and every hill is worth dying on. For others, flight is the answer. Every time. They never find the confrontation muscle, forsaking those they should defend and never calling a bluff. They will never die in a fight, but they will never stand firm for anything.

Abram demonstrates there is a time to fight and a time to leave. He risked his own life to rescue others. There is a time to fight—just not every time. He fought kings, but he fought to rescue the bound. The king he did not fight was the king of Sodom. In the presence of a king such as Sodom's, our lives are at risk. However, the answer is not to fight but to flee. Leave with nothing, keep nothing, and never look back.

CHAPTER 3

Moses and a God of Deliverance

Afterward Moses and Aaron went to Pharaoh and said, "This is what the LORD, the God of Israel, says: 'Let my people go....'" Pharaoh said, "Who is the LORD, that I should obey him and let Israel go?..." Then they said, "The God of the Hebrews has met with us. Now let us...offer sacrifices to the LORD our God, or he may strike us with plagues or with the sword."

—Exodus 5:1–3

THERE IS A heroic aspect to prophetic ministry, especially when the prophets confront the "kings" of this earth. It takes no small amount of courage to stand before the world's power systems and speak the word of God. When that word becomes a word of rebuke or correction or even a God-ordered change of direction, the courage level required is beyond the imagination of most.

Think again of the two Methodist ministers in 1785, delivering what amounted to a prophetic challenge to George Washington. It took some serious Holy Ghost courage to beseech a slave-owning president to outlaw slavery. Certainly, they were in no physical danger. Washington was a good and decent man despite being a slave owner. He wasn't going to have those ministers arrested or executed, and they knew that. Still, most would not have been so bold calling on the general to take so great a step. Nor would most have been so prophetic as to see the moral and historical importance of such a confrontation.

Prophetic ministry in its bravest form is the voice of divine confrontation against resistant world forces. Do not think for a moment that it is fun. Do not think that it is without cost or danger. God has called and still calls individuals and the church to confront societal and individual evil in the form of human rulers—and these confrontations are often hinges of history.

I believe there have been four major crossroads in American history in which the church attempted to speak prophetically to the nation and its leaders. The first was the epic confrontation over the abolition of slavery. Though many Christians failed to make known the judgment of

God on the institution of slavery, others spoke prophetically in His name and for His glory. Many at that contentious time said, "In Christ we cannot own human beings or deprive them of life and liberty."

Most abolitionists were Christians, one in particular being Julia Ward Howe. To the tune of "John Brown's Body," she wrote what would become the battle hymn of the Union troops in America's great Civil War. When you read the lyrics of this magnificent song, you are reading an incarnational, prophetic statement.

Mrs. Howe said: "I see God in the watchfires of the Union Army. When I look on the hillsides and see a thousand Union campfires, I see the hand of God." Then she said that God "is trampling out the vintage where the grapes of wrath are stored." In the marching boots of the Union army, they trampled out the vintage. In Sherman's march from Atlanta to Savannah, they just about burned Georgia to the ground. She said, "That's God. For all of the slavery and all of the evil that has been stored up year after year after year—for all of the wickedness that has been done in the name of the economy of the South, the Union Army is the punishing hand of God."

This must have been infuriating for Southerners to hear. Yet today, amazingly, "The Battle Hymn of the Republic" is sung in Southern churches. We have moved beyond the prophetic battle over the abolition of slavery, thanks be to God.

The second major prophetic battle in American society, one that continues to wage to this day, is against alcohol and drugs. Our nation attempted a legal fix for this crisis with Prohibition in the early twentieth century. This effort led to a doomed and misguided amendment to the Constitution, which did not solve anything. Still, perhaps the greatest and noblest part of this effort was that churches stood up in their prophetic might and declared that it is wrong for people to drink themselves to death and thus condemn both themselves and their families to destruction. People of God rose up, as they often do today, and proclaimed that addiction to alcohol and drugs is not of God and completely opposed it. This was a necessary battle. It was, and still is, a godly battle. Prohibition was a misguided and failed legal instrument, but a prophetic church cannot acquiesce to the horrors of alcoholism and drug addiction and those who profit from both.

The third major prophetic battle that has raged in the United States was the battle to end the wickedness of segregation. After the nation abolished the institution of slavery, Jim Crow laws in the South institutionalized the degradation of Blacks. Many forget that the opposition to Jim Crow was largely a prophetic movement of the church. I realize that not all churches rose up in righteous fury. In fact, many supported segregation. Yet Dr. Martin Luther King captured this moment in his heartrending *Letter From Birmingham Jail*. He said, flatly, that this business of segregation was wrong, ungodly, and destructive. He boldly accused the white, evangelical, "blood-washed," Bible-believing Christian preachers who refused to stand up and denounce segregation. He was right to do this, and he was prophetic. This was a time of lynchings, but beyond the numbers there was the daily nightmare of a million petty customs and laws used to beat a race into humiliating submission.

Even though Prohibition failed as a legal solution, the backbone of segregation was broken legally. Though individual racism will never be stamped out this side of heaven, the legal and financial systems of America are not what they were in the past, a barrier to an entire race. That boil has been lanced, and it was largely due to prophetic voices in the church.

Finally, we are now embroiled in yet another great moral battle, yet another prophetic contest in which the church has taken the lead. This is the battle against abortion. I'll tell you frankly that this battle should never have been necessary. It seems that anyone with a beating heart would know that crushing children in the womb or, in some cases, killing them outside of the womb just after birth, is evil at a historic level. It is a demonic, genocidal mania, a level of wickedness that has the effect of wiping out future generations and perverting an entire society. Yet we have had to fight this battle because not everyone is convinced— not in the world, not in American society, and not even in the church. Therefore, the prophetic church fights on, as it should.

How do these four struggles relate to Moses? Quite obviously, on the one hand. Yet there are subtle differences worth considering. One major difference between the battles Moses was called to fight and the moral battles in American history is divine motive. It is true that both required bold confrontation, both required courage, and both were prophetic in nature. Yet God, through Moses, wasn't trying to eradicate a national evil. Moses stated a very personal message from the living God: *These are My people. Let them go!*

This is important. The conflict between Moses and Pharaoh was not specifically about the institution of slavery as a social evil. Slavery certainly is evil, but that was not at the heart of the conflict. It is likely there were other slaves in Egypt's vast empire at the time, yet God did not order Egypt to end the practice of slavery. Moses' message was specific. Release the Hebrew slaves. The point is that this was not a generalized conflict between good and evil. This was about God's people, whom Pharaoh claimed as his own. The question was quite simply, To whom did the Hebrews belong—God or Pharaoh?

The God of the Hebrew people raised up a prophet whose life story was the most unlikely of them all and put in his mouth one message: "The God of Abraham wants His people back. Egypt has had them long enough." The only person who could make the decision to free God's people was Pharaoh himself, and he steadfastly refused. That made it personal: God versus Pharaoh. Only one could be right. Only one could be the Lord of the Hebrews. Because Moses was the prophet who delivered the message, and probably because of Moses' personal history in Egypt nearly half a century earlier, the conflict became, at another level, between Moses and Pharaoh.

Moses never denounced slavery, nor did he rebuke Egypt for its idolatry. This was a grudge match about who had the right to choose the destiny of the Hebrew people. Pharaoh was not about to give up his authority easily. The Hebrews were his, he believed. He alone could choose where they lived, or indeed which of them lived. He decided what they ate and what their labors would be. Pharaoh didn't just rule their wretched, purposeless lives. More importantly, he stood between them and their destiny as a people, as a "nation"—which they had never before been and which few held any hope of becoming. They were his slaves, and their only destiny was to work their lives away for his enrichment and die in the ghettos of Goshen.

This was Pharaoh's claim. This was his intention. Yet according to Moses, the Hebrews were God's people and God had a higher purpose and better place for them. Their destiny was not Pharaoh's to decide, nor did it lie in the slime pits of Egypt.

The Moses-Pharaoh clash was head to head, eyeball to eyeball, and man to man—or at least man to man of God. This had nothing to do with cleansing the moral climate of Egypt. This was about one simple question: Who owned the Hebrew people? Who got to make the big decisions about them? No compromise was possible. This was a bilateral, nonnegotiable, win-lose conflict from which only one victor could emerge.

The conflict between the prophet Moses and the pharaoh was never an attempt to reform Egypt's king or culture. There was no call to repentance, no blazing denunciation of Egypt's public idolatry or of Pharaoh's secret sins, whatever they might have been. The burden of Moses' message to Pharaoh was direct and clear: "Thus saith the Lord, let My people go."

Pharaoh's response was equally clear and no less direct: "The Hebrews belong to me, not to some long-forgotten and impotent slave god. They are mine, and I will not be deprived of them at the word of an elderly fallen prince who, after forty years, returns to Egypt from the deep desert. Who is this old man to tell me that what has been Egypt's for four hundred years is no longer mine? No. Mine the Hebrews have been, and mine they will remain."

With that the die was cast. Prophet versus Pharaoh, the God of Abraham versus the gods of Egypt. And the prize was a people in slavery and a nation not yet born.

Like Samuel's story, Moses' begins with the story of a woman. You may recall that Samuel's begins with his mother's barrenness and her desire for a child. The story of Moses is not about a barren woman. It's about the sacrifice made by a mother. You remember that his mother had her baby during the time of Egyptian bondage when a terrible law required that all the Hebrew male babies be killed.

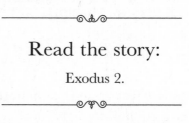

Read the story:

Exodus 2.

This is a hard story for us to absorb. We have to picture midwives strangling newborn babies; we have to imagine children killed at birth.

I suppose none of this is too shocking for people who live in America today, because we are doing much the same. We sanitize the discussion a bit, of course. We call such things "post-birth abortions." This is just a nice way of saying infanticide. We practice this today in America, so it is not asking too much for us to picture the infanticide demands that fell upon Moses' mother.

When she gave birth to Moses, she hid him. In time, as he grew, there was no place to hide him. So this agonized mother made a terrible decision. She put Moses in a basket and hid him in the reeds of the Nile. You know the story. Moses' sister, Miriam, watches as Pharaoh's daughter finds the baby in the basket and takes him as her own. Miraculously, Moses' mother is appointed to care for the child.

Moses, by the way, is not a Hebrew name; it is Egyptian. Perhaps you recall studying Egyptian history in high school and you remember encountering the name Thutmose. When you take away the *Thut* from that name, you have Mose, or Moses. This was his Egyptian name. In Hebrew, it was Moshe. In Arabic, it was Musa. Keep in mind that Moses is a prophet not only to the Jews and the Christians but also to Muslims. So he's internationally and transreligiously a prophet.

Moses was raised, then, in the household of Pharaoh, which is a divine comedy, is it not? Is that not a sublime joke? Pharaoh orders that the Hebrew babies all be murdered, and God says, "Here, raise this one." When he is a grown man, Moses, acting in the flesh, commits manslaughter. I don't think it can be called murder exactly, legally, but it is certainly manslaughter and against an Egyptian overlord, one of the slave masters. So Moses then flees and goes to Midian, where he marries a Midianite woman and works forty years for his father-in-law.

Interestingly, Moses' life was actually 120 years divided into three precise 40-year segments. He spent 40 years in Egypt. Then he spent 40 years in Midian. Finally, there were his 40 years wandering in the desert with the Hebrew people. God often works in the lives of His servants in just such a proportional, almost mathematical way.

What is important for our purposes is that Moses ultimately returned to Egypt from his self-imposed exile in the desert of Midian. The transition point between Midian and Egypt was the experience of the burning bush. Moses' summons into the office of prophet was supernatural in every way. With the possible exception of Isaiah, Moses' call was the most amazing. He saw the angel of the Lord in a bush that did not burn. He was experiencing the revelation of God as holy fire. Furthermore, he heard God's self-revelation as I Am. Moses was called to speak for a God whose character and nature was unchanging, eternal holiness. God is never "I was." He is never "I will be." He is "I am."

This experience at the burning bush is important for Moses. It is the commission that sends him back to Egypt and into Pharaoh's presence. Yet a distinction needs to be made. What Moses learned at the burning bush was a great lesson of God's character. He is I Am. He is holy. He is other. He is above all men and above all other gods. Yet when Moses goes to Pharaoh, he does not attempt to convince Pharaoh of God's nature. He is not attempting to introduce Pharaoh to who God is. The prophetic message of Moses is not apologetics. He is intending only to declare God's power.

The revelation of God's nature is not for Pharaoh. It is for the Hebrews held in captivity. To the people of God, Moses declares God's holiness, His complete and awesome otherness. They are meant to reclaim this faith and carry it with them out of Egypt into the Promised Land.

Our concern, though, is with Pharaoh and Moses' encounter with him. God is dealing with Egypt, not a Jewish king. Pharaoh is Egyptian. He's a pagan. He believes in all the gods and goddesses of Egypt. God is not trying to deal with a Jewish king of Israel or Judah. He isn't trying to teach Egypt who Jehovah is. He's simply trying to make Pharaoh obey Him. In fact, He's not even calling Pharaoh to repentance. He isn't concerned with Pharaoh's sin. Nor is He concerned about slavery as an institution. No; He's concerned about His people. He wants His people free so that they can worship Him and return to the Land. He wants Pharaoh to let His people go. This is the heart of the confrontation between Moses and Pharaoh.

We should take a moment and consider the nature of Moses in all of this. One of the principal points I'm eager to make in these pages is that prophets are not perfect. This is certainly true of Moses. He was, as the kids would say today, way not perfect! Moses had two major weaknesses. One was a temper, and the other was self-pity. On the surface these seem to be opposite problems, but they are actually related. A person with a self-pity problem might wallow in it and never explode. Moses wallowed from time to time but exploded when he couldn't stand it anymore. In fact, he struggled with his temper the whole time he led the Hebrews. It led to his crime of manslaughter. It led to his disobedience to God, time and again. Yet through all of this, one overriding strength set Moses on the high path and allowed God to use him: he is the meekest man who ever lived.

Meekness is one of the most misunderstood of all Christian virtues. Meekness is not weakness. It's power under control. My favorite illustration of this comes from watching the National Geographic channel. Recently there was a depiction of a mother lion, a lioness, who had three cubs. These little ones were climbing all over her and biting her ear and her leg. Now, this mother lion could have snapped any of those babies' necks with a swipe of her paw. She was that powerful. Instead, she picked them up and carried them safely in her massive jaw. God only knows what the pounds-per-square-inch pressure of a lion's jaw is. I'm sure it's terrifying. Yet this mother lion never hurt them. This may sound strange to you, but that mother lion was meek. Why? You cannot really display the virtue of meekness unless you have power. When great power is fully under control, fully tempered, you have meekness. So, Moses was a terrifyingly powerful man, but he was meek because that power was in check. That power could be made as gentle as a mother lion's jaw carrying her young.

Moses returns from Midian forty years after he has committed manslaughter, and he walks straight to Pharaoh, the most powerful king on earth. The Bible doesn't explain this. It just states it. What does it mean? Does Moses have access because of his past connection to the court? Maybe. On the other hand, his last and final connection to the court was criminal. There's probably a price on his head. So this is clearly a work of God, though we are left to ponder it, as I have done, without any clear answer. This is not a phenomenon just in the life of Moses. Nearly every biblical prophet seems able to simply walk into the courts of the kings they are meant to address. It is a feature of their ministry, a part of the empowerment they have for what they do. This should be encouraging to us. When God calls, He grants the access that the calling requires. This is surprising and thrilling at the same time.

Let's look more closely at the character and nature of Moses' conflict with Pharaoh. It is interesting that the contest with Pharaoh actually pushes Pharaoh into sin. The conflict is not initially about his sin. Yet as he hardens his heart and refuses to obey God, those actions become his sin. So what does this mean? It means the judgment on Egypt, and on Pharaoh personally, is a byproduct of the prophetic mission of Moses. Notice that God does not send Moses to say, "Repent and believe on Jehovah. Renounce slavery and God will bless you." No. It's not about that. The message is "Let My people go." When Pharaoh doesn't, he hardens his heart against obedience to God. That heart condition and resistance to the true God become the target of judgment.

An interesting question arises here. Does God punish Pharaoh for 430 years of slavery? Is He punishing Egypt for the slavery or for the disobedience of not letting Israel go when He says to let them go? I would say the answer is yes. Both are true.

Pharaoh's refusal to let God's people go brings the wrath of God on him, and this includes punishment for the sin of enslaving Israel from the beginning. This illustrates an important feature of prophetic confrontation. A prophet speaks the word of God. If a king resists, then judgment comes for far more than what the prophet was initially addressing. Resistance to God in one arena is answered with judgment for all that has been contrary to the will of God. This is why God's judgments seem so vast in the lives of nations. Resist God, anger Him on one point, and His wrath falls on all that has offended Him. To me, this makes prophets terrifying figures and the word of the Lord something to heed at all costs.

Yet our emphasis on Egypt is a bit misguided, isn't it? Moses is not about Egypt. His message is not really about Egypt. It's about God's people. The truth is that Moses is not speaking to a nation. Why? Because there is no nation of Israel yet. There is only the Hebrew people. There's no understanding of Israel in Egypt. Even the people themselves have no concept of being the nation of Israel. They are still emerging from slavery and a slave mentality.

Keep in mind that when the Hebrew people went into Egypt 430 years before Moses, they were only seventy in number. This was the family of Jacob.[1] Yet 430 years later, there were an estimated 2.5 million, all born in slavery. They've never known anything but slavery. So there is not a nation, there is only a slave-born tribe. Moses, then, is not really addressing Pharaoh as a person or calling him to repentance, and he's not really dealing as a prophet *to* Israel. He is, instead, the prophetic mechanism to take the Hebrew people out of bondage and toward Eretz Yisrael, the Land of Israel.

So the entire focus of Moses' ministry is to get the Hebrew people out of Egypt and to the Land that God gave their fathers. Remember that God always phrases His description of the Promised Land this way: "the Land that I gave to Abraham and Isaac." The Land is Eretz Yisrael, Hebrew for "the Land of Israel." Moses has one solitary

OF KINGS AND PROPHETS

task—the deliverance of the Hebrew people. This is why his ministry is so powerful. This is why it is so dramatic. And this is why the effect on Egypt is so devastating.

Let me use a modern parallel to make a deeper point about what we are examining by looking back at Germany at the end of World War II. Here is a terrifying truth: In an hour and a half, there were more Allied bombs dropped on Dresden, Germany, than were dropped on London during the entire Battle of London. During all those months when Nazis bombed London, a stunning number of bombs were dropped and there was horrible suffering. Yet a greater number were dropped by the Allies on Dresden in an hour and a half. It was a nightmare. And this was not all the suffering Germany endured. When Russia invaded Berlin at about the same time, there were atrocities committed that are too vile for me to recount here. There were bombings, fires, and death, of course. But then there was the very personal vengeance of the Russian soldiers. Germany is still feeling the agony of that time to this day.

But why did it all occur? Why were there such horrors visited on the German people? I'll tell you exactly why. You touch the Jews, you put your finger in the eyeball of God. We should fear for any nation that touches the Jewish people. This is what befell Egypt. Yes, Moses was liberating the Hebrew people, but when Pharaoh chose to resist God's command, he brought the most unimaginable horrors upon his people. So it has always been with God's defense of the Jews. So it will always be.

This is at the heart of the contest between Moses and Pharaoh, between the prophet of God and the ruler of Egypt. It's the quintessential contest between prophet and king. Pharaoh depended on an army, but God said, "I can drown your army in a minute." Pharaoh depended on magic, but God said, "I don't do magic tricks, but I can devour your magicians."

One of the greatest confirmations of Jehovah's superiority came in the plague in which Moses touched the sand with his staff and turned each grain into a gnat or perhaps lice (the Hebrew term can refer to either). Pharaoh then turns to his magicians and says, "OK, what about this one? You threw your staffs down and they became snakes. Can you match what Moses has done now?" But of course they could not, saying, "This is the finger of God." This phrase is a Hebrew idiomatic expression that actually means "the Holy Spirit."

This is important. Remember that terrible drunken orgy held by Belshazzar? The finger of God appeared in the sky and then wrote on a wall, "MENE, MENE, TEKEL, PARSIN... God has numbered the days of your reign and brought it to an end....You have been weighed on the scales and found wanting....Your kingdom is divided and given to the Medes and the Persians."[2] That's the finger of God.

Later in the story of Moses, the Ten Commandments were written in stone. By what? The finger of God, the Holy Spirit. So, those Egyptian magicians recognized that this was a power, a force, they couldn't duplicate or deal with or even fathom. The magicians were obviously practicing magic. They were playing tricks. Yet Moses was operating in the power of the Holy Spirit. And here, my friends, is the quintessential example of the conflict between prophetic power in the name of Jehovah God and kingly power in the name of an earthly realm.

Kings and political leaders tend to be high-octane, choleric achievers. Prophets tend toward the melancholy side of life. David, Jehu, Jehoshaphat—they were all about change, leading change, accomplishment, building, and numbers. They were hard driving, determined, and focused. Their vision was practical—building an army, building a nation, building Jerusalem, and building their dynasty. This tends to be the way leadership works in the natural domain.

Prophets, on the other hand, tend to be more on the melancholy side. They are deeply spiritual and highly sensitive. They are often happier alone with God than they are with people. Elijah struggled with this. Do you remember when the powerful prophet Elijah, who had just prayed down fire and killed 450 priests of Baal, sat all alone under a tree praying to die? Jeremiah was made of the same stuff. He's called the weeping prophet. This brings us to Moses. He was probably one of the strangest choices for a prophetic leader imaginable. Moses became to the Hebrew people what Samuel would later be as a judge. Moses was almost like a king himself. He led the people. He was the king of a movable nation in the desert. In fact, the New Testament calls the people at that time a church. They were like a church on the move. Was he a pastor, a prophet, a king, a ruler, or a judge? In a way, Moses was all of these. And yet he was previously content for forty years in the Midianite desert. You could say that God messed up Moses' life. Moses was married and happy tending his sheep. Then comes the burning bush, and from that day on Moses constantly intones, "Oh God, deliver me of these people!" This is the cry of a prophet.

Jesus Himself shows us the uniqueness of what it means to be a prophet. He was deeply sensitive, deeply spiritual. Often, He had to flee the people following Him. They swarmed Him. There was a constantly boiling, seething mass of people around Jesus, pulling on Him, calling to Him: "Save me, touch me, heal me." "Here's my daughter; raise her from the dead!" People with needs moved in a throng around Him. So great was this ever-present crowd that one time in the middle of the night Jesus went to the top of a mountain just to get away from the people. He allowed the disciples to leave ahead of Him by boat just so He could have a moment alone. Later, He had to walk on water just to catch up with them.

In short, prophets are simply odder than kings. There is an oddness, a strangeness about prophets. They are not people who have vast quantities of friends and relationships. They are unique, and they stand out in their generation. Yet because of their isolation and willingness to be odd, they impact their age by proclaiming the will of the living God.

LESSONS FROM OLD DR. MARK ABOUT MOSES

Never claim for yourself what belongs to God.

Learn this one lesson, this one great lesson, and life can be blessed. Never underestimate the unspeakable misery that can befall your life and the lives of others by refusing to learn it.

This was Pharaoh's horrific mistake. The Hebrews belonged to God. Likewise, your life belongs to God. Claim to be your own and you are stealing yourself from God. That is what makes abortion such a horrible sin. A woman who commits an abortion is stealing two lives from the ownership of God—hers and her unborn baby's. Killing the baby is a terrible sin, but that sin is the result of another previous sin, which is the theft of the baby from God.

The woman says, "It's my body and it's my baby. I can do whatever I choose with both." Thereby hangs the tale. Neither are hers. Both lives belong to God. To kill the baby, she must first claim both it and the body that hosts it as hers. That is exactly what Pharaoh said, "These Hebrews are mine, and I have the power of life and death over them." God said, "They are Mine, and you are a thief and a murderer. They are not yours, but a world of horrific pain is yours." Stealing from God is the passageway to agony.

Do not confuse failed methods with false ministry.

Moses' initial attempt to help his Hebrew brethren was misguided to say the least. It resulted in the death of an Egyptian soldier and Moses' own forty-year exile. However, that false start did not mean Moses was a false prophet. Have you had a false start? OK, then go back to the point of your calling. Start again...back there. Have you been sidelined like Moses was? Let God get you back on the field in His way and in His time, and when He does, do it God's way this time. That's about as clear and simple as it can be. An authentic calling is not always a fail-safe insulation from a bad beginning, but a bad beginning does not necessarily have to mean a bad ending.

Nobody sins in a vacuum.

The contest between God and Pharaoh was personal. Both claimed to own the Hebrews. The issue was Pharaoh's stubborn narcissism, his personal rebellious sin, and his rejection of Moses' prophetic ministry. Pharaoh sinned personally. Yet all of Egypt suffered. No one sins in a vacuum. Spouses, families, churches, and even nations suffer when leaders sin. The drunk who drives is not in a vacuum. The corrupt politician may tell himself the bribe he takes hurts no one else, but it does. No false accusation is made in a vacuum. Reputations, careers, marriages, and families get damaged. Sin hurts people other than just the sinner. The firstborn baby boy of an Egyptian mother wailed in the night as it died in her arms, but it was Pharaoh's sin that killed him, not hers.

CHAPTER 4

Samuel and the Kingdom of Israel

Samuel called to Saul on the roof, "Get ready, and I will send you on your way." When Saul got ready, he and Samuel went outside together. As they were going down to the edge of the town, Samuel said to Saul, "Tell the servant to go on ahead of us…but you stay here for a while, so that I may give you a message from God."

—1 Samuel 9:25–27

I WAS BORN IN a small town in northeast Texas, which led to many wonderful things in my life. One of them was that, along with many other Texans, I embraced Sam Houston as a beloved hero and radiating influence.

Sam Houston is far more of an international and historical figure than most people realize. He is the only man in the history of the United States who was the governor of two states. He is also the only man not only to be the head of a foreign country but to hold the position twice, in addition to serving in both the US House of Representatives and the US Senate. There's much more. His life was one of adventure. As a young boy, he ran away from home and lived with the Cherokee Indians. He was adopted by a Cherokee chief and given the name The Raven, a name that remained with him all his days. He is one of the few men in history to have fought in the armies of two different nations. He was wounded several times, including once while fighting in the Creek War and again during his great victory at San Jacinto.

Later in his life, Houston was a national and international celebrity, particularly in Texas. Texans adored him—until the issue of secession arose. Houston opposed secession. He traveled up and down the state of Texas— by that time it had ceased being the Republic of Texas— preaching his view that secession would be bad for Texas and bad for the United States. In town after town, frontier community after frontier community, he poured out his fierce beliefs but was shouted down and voted down again and again. Finally, when as governor he was required to sign the oath of allegiance to the Confederacy, he refused. He was deposed, kicked out of office by the people of Texas.

In the spring of 1861 he spoke out, again defending the principles that had cost him so much. You can feel Houston's agony, his grief over the future of the state and the nation he loved and had served so faithfully.

> Friends have warned me that my life was in great peril if I expressed my honest sentiments and convictions. But the hiss of the mob and howls of their jackal leaders can not deter me, nor compel me, to take the oath of allegiance to a so-called confederate government....The soil of our beloved south will drink deep the precious blood of our sons and brethren....I can not nor will not close my eyes against the light and voice of reason. The die has been cast by your secession leaders...and you must ere long reap the fearful harvest of conspiracy and revolution.[1]

A few days later, in Galveston, Texas, looking down on a hostile crowd from a hotel balcony, he declared again:

> Some of you laugh to scorn the idea of bloodshed as the result of secession. But let me tell you what is coming....You may, after the sacrifice of countless millions of treasure and hundreds of thousands of lives, as a bare possibility, win Southern independence, if God be not against you, but I doubt it....The North is determined to preserve this Union....When they begin to move in a given direction, they move with the steady momentum of a mighty avalanche. My fear is, they will overwhelm the South.[2]

For declaring views such as these he was rejected. The great Sam Houston, once beloved by the people of Texas, was shunned. He died alone and despised in Huntsville,

Texas, at the age of seventy. The year was 1863—the mid-point of the great conflagration he had foreseen befalling the nation.

At the end of an incredible career of international military and political fame, what he predicted about the Civil War turned out to be exactly correct. None of this is to say that Sam Houston was a prophet. Making a prophetic statement in no way makes you a prophet. Yet the fact that he was right and ahead of his time did not keep him from losing everything he had and dying in exile, dishonored by his people.

It was much the same with the prophet Samuel. His death as described in Scripture is likewise unspectacular. He was not as lonely, forgotten, and despised as Sam Houston, but his death was just as overlooked. Scripture says, "And Samuel died."[3] The verse then tells us that Israel lamented him and buried him at his home. Certainly, he was mourned by many of the people in Israel, but there was no state funeral. There was no fancy tomb. Samuel died. Just that.

What he had prophesied about the problems that a king would bring to the country was stunningly accurate. When the people demanded a king, Samuel said, "God will give you a king if you want a king." But he said, "I'm telling you, you'll regret it." I wonder whether, when Samuel was on his deathbed, anyone came to him and said, "Old man, you were right. We're so sorry that we demanded a king. Saul was everything bad that you predicted he would be. Please, before you die, forgive us." I doubt this ever happened. I doubt that he got one single deathbed apology.

Let's look at the making of this prophet. Samuel was one of the greatest of all the prophets, as well as one of the earliest and the most powerful. His interactions with several kings give us essential insight into the conflict between prophets and kings. The story of this great prophet begins, as they all do, with a woman.

Samuel's mother, Hannah, was married to Elkanah. This detail may seem insignificant, but it was important to Rashi. Remember that I'm using a list of prophets formulated by a Jewish rabbi in the twelfth century, a man called Rashi. He examined the Scriptures and formulated a list of all the prophets. Some on his list are famous, like Abraham. Some would surprise you. For example, he lists Hannah and Elkanah as prophets. They are the parents of Samuel. Since they gave birth to a prophet, they are honored among the prophets.

Read the story:

1 Samuel 1.

Hannah was barren. Peninnah, wife number two, humiliates Hannah, a cruelty that is repeated in several stories throughout the Old Testament—and to a certain extent in the New Testament. Hannah, like Sarah, cries out to the Lord. She vows that if the Lord were to give her a child, she would dedicate him to God for all his life. The Lord grants her prayer, and when Hannah realizes she is pregnant, she does indeed dedicate her baby to God, at least partially as a Nazarite. There are other similarities to familiar biblical stories. Samson's mother, for example, dedicated her son as a Nazarite. Elizabeth dedicated John the Baptist as a Nazarite too.

———

It is important we know what a Nazarite was, as they were not necessarily prophets and not all prophets—few of them, in fact—were Nazarites. The Nazarites were a dedicated order of highly devoted men who took important vows, including that they could not drink wine. In fact, the vow was so severe that a Nazarite was not to even enter a vineyard or touch a grape. They also never cut their hair. They were to live holy, set-apart lives. These vows were not easy to keep. Samson, of course, failed miserably in his vows. John the Baptist kept his. Samuel also kept his, though only one—not cutting his hair—is ever mentioned.

There is another important theme in the story of Hannah. Scripture says, "And Hannah prayed and said, 'My heart exults in the LORD; my horn is exalted in the LORD. My mouth derides my enemies.'" Who would this enemy be? It's her husband's other wife. "My mouth derides my enemies, because I rejoice in your salvation. There is none holy like the LORD: for there is none besides you; there is no rock like our God."[4]

Does this language sound familiar? It should. In it we hear the song that Mary sang when she learned she was pregnant: "My soul magnifies the Lord, and my spirit rejoices in God my Savior, for he has looked on the humble estate of his servant. For behold, from now on all generations will call me blessed; for he who is mighty has done great things for me, and holy is his name. And his mercy is for those who fear him from generation to generation."[5]

In addition to the similarities between Hannah and Mary, there is also a similarity between Hannah and Elizabeth. Their sons, Samuel and John the Baptist, are similar. There is a parallel between Hannah and the mother of Samson because both children were Nazarites. Finally, there is the common experience of Hannah and Sarah because Sarah had conflict with Hagar, and Hannah is tortured by Peninnah. Each of these parallels hints to us of the prophetic purposes of Hannah's child. Each signals what we are to look for in the story.

———

It is important that we understand the setting for the next episode of Hannah's life. She goes to Shiloh where Eli the high priest is and where the ark of the covenant also rests. She is so passionate before God as she prays that she is kneeling, rocking back and forth, and praying with great energy. You have likely seen people praying in the same way if you have visited the Western Wall in Jerusalem. Hannah's style of praying is multiplied there by the thousands. Jews rock back and forth, pouring out their heartfelt petitions to God. Yet so passionate is the prayer offered there that it has come to be known mistakenly as the Wailing Wall.

This helps us understand Hannah. She is tortured by Peninnah. She feels as if she's nothing. She is agonizing in prayer, rocking back and forth and soundlessly moving her lips as she makes her heart known to God. Eli notices her. He assumes she is drunk and rebukes her. He says, "You showed up here drunk? What are you doing? Why won't you give up this drunkenness and change your life?" She responds, "I'm not drunk. I'm passionate for the Lord. I'm crying out for a baby." And so Eli, who is on the list of Rashi's prophets, says, "Go home. You're going to have a baby."

———

There's a fascinating little passage in Hannah's prayer to God. At one point she says the phrase "LORD of hosts." This is the first time this name for God is used in the Bible, and it's said by a woman. Does it mean the heavenly host or multitude? Angels? The vast host of the stars that God has created? Or God of the host of all the Jewish people?

One of the rabbinical writers makes an interesting comment about this. He believes Hannah is accusing the Lord: "You're a God of many, You're a God of the host of angels, You're a God of the host of the stars, You're a God of the host of the Jewish people, and You won't even give me one?" This rabbi says that she "hurls" these words at God.[6]

How fascinating! Here is an important truth. Our God is a big God. If you have ever come to that moment when you have hurled your words at God, trust me, He is OK with it. He's not going to be mad at you. He's not going to kill you. It's all right. You can pour your heart out in all honesty to God. He actually loves it because such prayer is an approach to intimacy with Him, almost a face-to-face relationship, which is exactly what God wants. It is also a characteristic of some down-to-earth, Jewish, nonliturgical praying.

Perhaps you've seen *Fiddler on the Roof.* It's the story

of Reb Tevye, a Jewish peasant at the time of the Russian pogroms, when there was much persecution of the Jews. Tevye talks to God throughout the movie as though he is addressing a kind of "big guy." Like the psalmist does at times, he confronts God with his complaints. At one point he's leading his horse home from delivering the milk, and the horse goes lame. Reb Tevye looks up at the sky and says, "Dear God, was that necessary? Did you have to make him lame just before the Sabbath? That wasn't nice. It's enough you pick on me....But what have you got against my horse? Really, sometimes I think, when things are too quiet up there, you say to yourself, 'Let's see. What kind of mischief can I play on my friend, Tevye?'"[7] This long-suffering character has an almost intimate interaction with God. Of course, this doesn't really line up with our theology. We know God is not in heaven deciding whose horse goes lame. Still, this is an interesting way to consider Hannah's prayer, a very confrontive prayer, which she hurls at God.

Nine months later, the baby is born. Hannah takes the toddler, Samuel, to Eli as soon as he's weaned. She has made a bargain with God: "If You'll give me a baby, I'll let him be raised in the tabernacle." In fulfillment of her vow, she entrusts Samuel to the high priest, who is to raise the boy as his own, as though Eli is a foster father who will train and teach him. Keep in mind that Samuel is a young boy.

We should know too that Eli has two natural sons, Phinehas and Hophni, who are moral and priestly failures. They are priests but they are corrupt and truly wicked.

One night, as Samuel is sleeping, he hears a voice call to him. He thinks it's Eli. He gets up and goes to Eli and he says, "Here I am; you called me." Eli says, "I did not call; go back and lie down."

The voice comes again: "Samuel!" And he gets up and goes to Eli. "Here I am; you called me."

"My son," Eli said, "I did not call; go back and lie down."

The third time the boy comes in and Eli catches on. He says, "Go and lie down, and if he calls you, say, 'Speak, LORD, for your servant is listening.'"[8] That is the beginning of Samuel's lifelong intimate and prophetic relationship with God.

It is interesting that Eli is listed in Rashi's prophets. I've pondered this often. Why would Eli be on that list? Is it because he identifies this little boy as being someone spiritually significant? Is it because he prophesies over Hannah that she will have a baby and the result is the great prophet Samuel? Perhaps it's all of these, but regardless of why, Eli is numbered among the prophets.

It is also interesting that when it comes to Eli, we have to recall one of the most important things we've learned about the prophets: great as they were, they also had failings. Eli in particular had deep failings. The most important was that he would not deal with his sons' sins.

During Eli's service as high priest, the Philistines attacked. Defeat was imminent. It seemed that everything would be lost. Eli's sons were tasked with carrying the ark of the covenant into the Israelite camp. As they did so, the Israelites started cheering. The Philistine response is fascinating: "A god has come into the camp," and they were terrified.[9]

At first the Philistines were intimidated by the sudden and unexpected enthusiasm among the Israelis. In their paganism the Philistines ascribed the cheering to the arrival of a god in the enemy camp. Finally, and unfortunately for the Israelis, a voice of calm encouragement prevailed. "Come on," he called out, "Fight like men!"[10] And fight they did. The joy among the Israelis at the arrival of the ark was short lived and gave way to utter disaster.

Please notice that we may think we will use momentary enthusiasm to intimidate the enemy, but it will not give us victory. All the cheering, all the volume, all the religious symbolism in the world cannot give us victory if God is not with us. The Philistines are initially intimidated by all the cheering. Then they realize it is just shouting, merely emotional—natural and without spiritual power. Mere noise is no way to win in spiritual warfare. There is no power in it, no victory. The Philistines go into battle and wipe them out. It is an utter tragedy. Phinehas and Hophni are killed, and the Philistines capture the ark of the covenant.

There is a vital lesson for us in this. Religious fervor, revving yourself up and getting excited, is not really much of a key to victory. It's pop joy. It doesn't change the outcome of the conflict. It isn't true warfare. Furthermore, it can be a distraction from the real battle.

There is an important side note in what happens next. Because of their great victory, the Philistines have the ark of the covenant. Yet God punishes them so severely for taking the ark that the Philistines send it back to the Israelites. There is a backstory here that we often miss in our English Bibles. Trust me, it is very clear in Hebrew. To put it bluntly, God gives the Philistines hemorrhoids. In fact, He gives them such horrible hemorrhoids that the Philistines realize they are under judgment and move to get rid of the dangerous object they have captured.

The humor of this is inescapable. However, the pain God gave the Philistines hardly alleviated the devastation that had befallen Israel. When the ark was taken and the battle was lost, Phinehas and Hophni were both killed. When Eli heard this, he fell backward, broke his neck, and died. Phinehas' wife, who was pregnant, went into labor due to the terrible defeat, the loss of the ark, and the deaths of her husband, father-in-law, and brother-in-law. She therefore named the baby Ichabod, "The Glory has departed."[11] No truer words could have been spoken. The battle had been lost. The ark of the covenant had been captured. The baby's father, grandfather, and uncle were dead. The glory had indeed departed Israel.

Nice name, right? Interestingly, the name Ichabod became famous in American culture because of the short story by Washington Irving called "The Legend of Sleepy Hollow." In this story, a harsh schoolteacher living in the American colonies is haunted by the legend of a soldier who lost his head in battle and is searching for it. The teacher's name is Ichabod Crane—that even sounds funny. The story is one of great humor and fun, but that name, Ichabod, should remind us of that moment in Israel's history when the glory had departed and a child was named Ichabod to memorialize the tragedy.

All these deaths. All this horrible, humiliating defeat. What good could possibly come of all this? The high priest and both his sons are dead. Who could possibly head Israel now? The answer to both questions is Samuel. Samuel is that good leader God will call to step forward.

———

Soon after this episode, there is a telling sentence about Samuel in the Bible: "The LORD was with him and let none of his words fall to the ground."[12] Not one word fell to the ground. This is what I pray for in preaching. Any good teacher or minister prays this. I've been in worship services when the sermon was spoken and then died a horrible death before it reached the front row. Preaching at its prophetic best goes straight to the hearts of the hearers. Not one word falls to the ground. This is perhaps the most important truth about Samuel's ministry. When he spoke, every word hit its target, and gradually the people of Israel began to grow in their confidence in Samuel.

We watch in Scripture as Samuel rises to become a sort of "triple threat" leader. He is a prophet. He also serves as a priest because he often offers sacrifice. He also acts as a judge. This is important since he appears in history at the end of the period of judges and just before the period of the kings. Remember, he parallels John the Baptist, who stood with one foot in the Old Testament and one in the New Testament. First, John announced that "Messiah will come." Then, he declared, "Messiah is here." In the same way, Samuel stands with one foot in the Book of Judges and one foot in the books of Samuel, Kings, and Chronicles. It is Samuel who ushers out the time of the judges and ushers in the era of the kings. Samuel is one of the greatest figures in Israel's history.

Samuel is there when the people rise up and say, "We want a king. We want to be like other nations. Give us a king. We don't want to have to hunt down a prophet and pray. Give us a king who'll lead us and formulate a government and formulate a nation. We want a king." Samuel says, "It's not going to be what you think. You think you want a king, but a king will draft your sons and put them in the army. If he wants your horses for his soldiers, he'll take them. Be careful what you ask for."

The people insist, though. "We want a king! We want a king!" Finally, God tells Samuel, "They're not rejecting you. They're rejecting Me."

Anytime the word of God is declared with power and anointing and the hearers get angry, they are rebelling not so much against the person who's preaching that word as they are the source of that word. This is both the pain and comfort of prophetic preaching. Anger and rejection may very well come, but the rejection is not the preacher's but the Lord's.

Likewise, God says to all who declare His truth, "Be humble. When they receive the word you preach, they aren't receiving you. Don't take too much credit for it."

Now we come to Samuel's interaction with Saul, the man chosen to be king. Remember that Samuel is tasked with anointing him. Saul has physical characteristics that commend him. He's the tallest man in the nation, head and shoulders taller than anyone else. If kings are supposed to be big and strong, Saul is perfect; he looks the part. Beyond his appearance, Saul has one great virtue not so common in kings. In fact, Saul steadfastly refuses to be king. He says, "No, I don't want to be the king!" and he hides among the suitcases and the baggage.[13] He keeps insisting, "I don't want to be the king, I'm not a king. I'm just a working stiff, I don't want this." His physical appearance and his humility combine to give Saul's reign a hopeful beginning. Beyond all that, he is, quite simply, God's choice, yet he is a disaster of a king.

This raises a problem, doesn't it? Is God mistaken about Saul? Is He wrong about how Saul will turn out? God doesn't make mistakes, does He? So how do we interpret this? Is God raising Saul up to punish Israel by giving them one who will turn out to be a bad king? It hardly seems likely that God would be petulant. In fact, this problem comes down to what we believe about free moral agency. In other words, is what God foreknows always immutable? Or can we change the chosen path by our actions? If God knows we're going to sin, can we choose not to sin? Or does His knowledge confine us?

Saul was not a moral puppet. He made his own choices and wrecked his own life. Just as we always make our own decisions. We always have freedom of choice. Even so, this story was always headed toward David's kingship. Saul was responsible for the ruin of Saul, but David was always the destination of the story.

Samuel anoints Saul and makes him king. Almost immediately a clash begins between the prophetic anointing on Samuel and the royal authority of Saul. When Saul is about to go to battle, Samuel declares, "I'll be there on the seventh day. Wait for me, and don't go into battle until I come and bring a sacrifice." Humility was Saul's virtue. Impatience and carnality were among his weaknesses. As the sun starts to sink, Saul panics. The day is almost over. Saul, ever impatient, offers the sacrifice. When Samuel arrives, he says, "What are you doing?" Saul replies, "You didn't come!" Samuel says, "I was on the way!"[14]

We would do well to remember what Saul forgot. Our God is an "on-time God." The biggest mistakes in the Bible, the ones with the greatest consequences, were made by people who would not wait on God. Rush ahead with your plan, as Abraham and Sarah did, and you may give birth to an Ishmael that will haunt you for the rest of your life. Always wait for God's timing no matter how nervous or impatient you become.

Samuel had also told Saul, "When you defeat the Amalekites, don't keep anything. Kill all the people, kill all the livestock, and burn all the goods. Don't keep anything. Burn it all." That kind of command is hard for us to stomach, but keep in mind that we're reading

Read the story:

1 Samuel 15.

an Old Testament story. From it we can draw this truth: God has the right to judge any of us at any moment. A person may think that he or she is going to get a long, lovely, healthy life with time for a lengthy deathbed repentance, but God can call anyone's ticket any time He wants to. Just as He called the ticket of the Amalekites. Samuel's prophetic command was clear: "The Amalekites are so wicked and so evil. Destroy them completely."

Samuel arrives at the scene of the battle and finds Saul has been victorious. Once there, Samuel asks, "Did you kill all the livestock like I told you?" What follows is like a Monty Python skit.

SAMUEL: Did you kill all the livestock like I told you?

SAUL: We sure did. We killed them all.

SAMUEL: Well, that's funny. I hear sheep.

SAUL: OK, well. All right, we did keep some of the sheep.

SAMUEL: Why did you keep some of the sheep?

SAUL: We're going to offer them as sacrifices. But we killed everything else.

SAMUEL: That's funny now because I hear cattle lowing.

SAUL: OK, OK, OK. We didn't kill all the cattle.

This is remarkable. It's like the conversations you probably have had with your teenager:

"Did you clean the house?"

"Absolutely."

"Why isn't this floor vacuumed?"

"Well, OK, I didn't vacuum this floor."

Samuel must be getting tired in this exchange:

SAMUEL: Well, what about the Amalekites? Did you kill them all?

SAUL: As to the Amalekites, we killed them—every one.

SAMUEL: OK. Who's in your tent?

SAUL: Well, the king. We kept the king.

SAMUEL: Agag is in your tent?

SAUL: Yes, we killed the rest of them, but I kept Agag. He's in my tent.

Picture the next moment with me. Samuel turns to Saul. He's angry. He's holding a sword. He says, "You've ruined it. You've ruined it! You disobeyed God." Saul pitifully responds, "I kept things only for sacrifice." This, of course, is a lie. He wasn't going to sacrifice the king, after all.

At this point Samuel speaks some of the most important words in the entire Bible: "Do you think that God cares more about sacrifice than He does about obedience? Rebellion is like witchcraft."[15] Why is this true? It's a fascinating prophetic statement to make to a king, who is a natural authority. *Rebellion* is a toxic word to any king. Rebellion that bypasses the king forms a kind of substitute power. That's mutiny. That's a rebellion. Samuel is saying, "What if somebody got an army and came against you? Isn't that rebellion? That's the same thing witchcraft is, because witchcraft bypasses the supernatural power and will of God to seek another pathway to power."

Samuel was making it clear to Saul: "You've done that to God, and this is like witchcraft. God is going to take your kingdom away from you and give it to somebody else who will do what He says." With that, Samuel the prophet simply turns to walk away. As he does, Saul grabs Samuel's robe and tears it. Under a prophetic anointing, Samuel turns back to Saul and says, "As you have ripped my garment, God has ripped the kingdom away from you."

Saul's response is intriguing. He doesn't even argue. He doesn't deny it. He just says, "OK. I accept that. But we don't have to tell everybody else. Just go out with me in front of the elders of the tribes of Israel and have a prayer with me." In other words, he is saying in essence, "The fact that God has departed from me and that I am in God's eyes no longer the king—fine. But let me be the king in the people's eyes. Let's just do this charade in front of the people."

Samuel's response is the one that I can't get over. We might think that he would say, "No, I'm not going to do that! No!" Instead, Samuel says, "OK. If that's all you want. You just want this outside show? You just want to be on the royal dais wearing the crown? You know it's hollow. You know it doesn't mean anything. You know God has removed it from you, right? You know that the real king is elsewhere. You know all that, and you just want to sit on the throne and wear the crown and me offer a prayer? OK."

After that Samuel does what Saul did not. He demands that Agag be brought to him, "and Samuel hacked Agag to pieces before the LORD in Gilgal."[16]

So how do we interpret this? I believe that God is a good God. He does not trick us just because we don't pray with exactly the right words. I also believe God will sometimes allow us to settle for the outward and superficial if that is all we want. If all you want is public acclaim, God may certainly allow you to have it. It is as though He is saying, "Is that all you want? You just want to be a big shot? You don't want to be the real deal? You just want to be a big deal? OK. If that's what you want, I'll let you be a big deal."

———

From that moment on, Saul is no longer the real king. He is king in name only. Samuel never speaks to him personally again and moves into a mysterious time of his life. He goes to Ramah, near Bethlehem. Remember that Samuel anointed Saul in the name of God. Now he has rejected Saul in the name of God. In Bethlehem, at the house of Jesse, he anoints Jesse's son David as the king.

Usually preachers and teachers focus this story on David. Try instead to see it from Samuel's point of view. What he's about to do is actually treason. There is already a king. A prophet who anoints a new king is guilty of sedition.

Likewise, keep in mind that Saul is the tallest man in the nation. David is the smallest son in Jesse's family.

Read the story:

1 Samuel 16:1–13.

I find it fascinating that because of this physical difference between the two men, even a prophet such as Samuel very nearly misses God. I have to confess that I love it when I read where prophets foul up. It gives me some small level of hope for my life!

Remember the scene. The sons of Jesse come in one by

one, six grown sons. And Samuel thinks, "OK, this is a great big strong guy. He's not quite as big, nor as strong as Saul. He doesn't look as royal as Saul, but he's close." So the natural impulse is to choose the man of natural kingly stature, the man who is as physically similar to Saul as possible. Yet God says, "That's not him." Then again, "That's not him. That's not him." This happens six times. Then Samuel asks Jesse, "Are these all the sons you have?" As if Jesse might have forgotten one. Jesse says, "OK, OK, there is another one. He's a weird kid. I will bring him in. But I just need to tell you, he's a very odd little duck." And the lad who is to become King David comes in from the field.

Keep in mind that David has not been in on anything up to this point. He doesn't know why Samuel is there. He doesn't know why this mysterious gathering is going on at his father's house. He is just a little sunburned boy. Picture the scene. He walks into his house and says, "Did you call me?" Suddenly an old man—a stranger to David—walks over to him, pours oil on his head, and then just walks away.

———

By this point in Samuel's story it is becoming increasingly obvious that he is a mysterious and somewhat fearful character. He is something of a dark, prophetic figure upon whom rests God's anointing. When he arrives at Bethlehem, the elders say, "Are you here to hurt us or help us?" They're thinking he could call down fire and kill them all. "Are you mad at Bethlehem? If you're mad, just tell us!" However, Samuel anoints David and leaves. The elders at Bethlehem are relieved. Interestingly, this is the last time that David and Samuel are together until David has to flee from Saul's presence.

———

I want to be careful to keep our cameras focused on Samuel and not on David. Still, we have to know David's story to know the context of Samuel's story. After David killed Goliath, he was promoted by Saul and then married Saul's daughter, Michal. In time Saul became jealous of David because of all his victories and his great acclaim among the people. Envy and fear gripped Saul, and he set himself to kill David.

Think about David's life beyond the headlines. He was just a boy when a weird old dude suddenly stepped into his life, anointed him as the king over Israel, and just as suddenly left. Sometime later through victory after amazing victory, David was a celebrity. Then his father-in-law's rage ripped the rug out from under him and David had to flee. He had been an international star, the son-in-law of the king, a celebrated hero. Nearly overnight he became an outlaw with a price on his head. Where can he go? He goes to Samuel, of course.

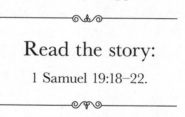

Read the story:

1 Samuel 19:18–22.

By this time Samuel is a fading star. Remember what I told you? He was prophet, priest, and judge. Now there's a king in Israel, and Samuel is an old man slipping slowly into obscurity. He's the aging Sam Houston. There's King Saul whom Samuel anointed. There's also a new king apparent whom Samuel had also anointed. During this dramatic, tumultuous time, what did Samuel do? He went to Ramah and opened a school to train prophets.

A retired Air Force officer once told me that there comes a moment where you quit flying planes and you start training pilots. As an old dude myself, that's precisely where I find myself. Somebody asked me, "Are you still pastoring a church?" I said, "Why, no. I'm in remission." This is not a time for me to pastor a church. I train pastors. I teach pastors. I lead and teach in the National Institute of Christian Leadership. I identify with Samuel in this latter stage of his life, though I do not identify with his prophetic anointing. That's because I have some level of sense!

I do understand Samuel, the aging prophet. He's fading, aging out. So he goes to Ramah and starts a school for prophets. It's kind of a mountain Bible school, and it's a little wild. When David is in crisis, he goes up there to hide out with Samuel. This is when one of the more supernatural scenes in the life of Samuel happens.

Saul finds out that David is up at Ramah with Samuel, so he sends soldiers to arrest David. When the soldiers arrive, they find David and Samuel with the other prophets. Strangely enough, the power of God comes on the soldiers and they begin to prophesy. The spirit of prophecy that's in Samuel's mountaintop school comes upon Saul's emissaries and they prophesy. They are not prophets, but they are prophesying. We don't know what they said, but presumably they're prophesying over David. They've come in to arrest him, but they end up declaring, "Blessed be David! God has raised you up to replace Saul!" At this, they tuck their tails between their legs and head back to King Saul.

Saul then sends another detachment of soldiers. The

same thing happens. He sends yet a third detachment of soldiers. The same thing happens again. Every time the soldiers return to Saul, he asks, "Did you kill him?" They say, "Well, OK now, see, Your Majesty, it's like, a very complicated scene up there." Finally, Saul says to himself, "If you're going to have somebody killed, you may as well do it yourself." So Saul takes a detachment of soldiers and goes up to Ramah himself. When Saul arrives, suddenly the same spirit of prophecy that had come on the soldiers comes on Saul. It's a bizarre scene. Saul takes off all his clothes. He strips naked and lies on the floor at David's feet. Saul, despite himself, prophesies. What a scene! Clearly, God is supernaturally protecting David in Samuel's presence. Keep in mind that Samuel is the center of this. His anointing is on the school, and his anointing now falls on Saul so that he lies on the floor all night prophesying God's purpose for David. None of this happens because David is present. It happens because Saul is in the presence of Samuel.

The final interaction between Saul and Samuel isn't an easy story to absorb. In fact, it is one of the most problematic passages in the

Read the story:

1 Samuel 28.

whole Bible, Old or New Testament. It has a kind of eeriness about it that feels more Shakespearean than biblical. Remember the witches' scenes in *Macbeth*: "Hail to thee, Thane of Cawdor"; "Double, double, toil and trouble"?[17] Remember how Macbeth meets those witches amidst the mist and the fog? This disturbing scene in Scripture is just that eerie. For us Christians, it's extremely hard to work through. Any teacher or writer who addresses it has a difficult time giving the story a full and satisfactory explanation.

Here is how it unfolds. Saul is about to fight his final awful battle with the Philistines. He knows this will be decisive, and he's terrified. If he wins, it will be a legendary victory. If he loses, he's going to die—the Philistines will kill him. He also knows that Samuel is dead. Samuel being deceased means King Saul can't get a word from God. He has no prophetic presence or leadership in his life. He tries to pray. Nothing comes to him. There can come a moment when you have stiff-armed God so long that God won't answer.

The words of Samuel are surely ringing in Saul's ears: "Rebellion is like witchcraft." Saul has been on a campaign throughout Israel to get rid of all the wizards, witches, magicians, and those with familiar spirits. Yet now he is desperate for supernatural information. At this moment, having done all that he could to cleanse the Land of witches and sorcerers, Saul goes to one himself.

Strange leads to strange in this story. Saul asks around: "Does anyone know where there's a woman with a familiar spirit?" The people reply, "There's a woman up in Endor." King Saul disguises himself and goes to the witch of Endor, demanding, "I want you to conjure up somebody for me." Amazingly, the witch replies, "Don't you know Saul has made this illegal? I'm not doing this because you're just trying to get me killed." Saul replies, "I promise you, no harm will come to you, and I will protect you. I promise you." The woman does not know who he is, so she agrees. Saul then says, "I want you to conjure up Samuel." He is asking her to engage in necromancy. Samuel is dead, and Saul is asking the witch to summon Samuel from beyond the grave. The witch's actual mechanics are not given to us, but whatever she does works. Suddenly Samuel appears. The witch has conjured a ghost.

The Bible tells us that when the witch sees Samuel, she also suddenly recognizes Saul. That doesn't make sense to us immediately, does it? Maybe Samuel appeared and said, "Hail, king of Israel." Maybe he bowed. We don't know how it happened. Yet when the witch sees Samuel and recognizes Saul, she becomes incensed. "You're Saul! You tricked me! You're going to kill me!" Saul answers, "I'm not going to kill you. I'm not going to hurt you! Tell me what you see." This is interesting because it implies that Saul cannot see the person, or ghost, the witch can see. She does as Saul asks and tells him what she is seeing: "I see an old man with a mantle." A mantle is a symbol of the office and anointing of a prophet.

This symbolism is so obvious that when this mantle is mentioned, Saul says, "It must be Samuel. It must be Samuel." At that point he speaks to Samuel, or to the spirit of Samuel. He asks, "What's going to happen tomorrow?" Samuel replies, "You're going to lose to the Philistines, and by this time tomorrow you and all your sons will be with me among the dead."

The next day Saul is indeed defeated on Mount Gilboa, and his decapitated body is hung on the walls of Beth Shan.

What does the whole strange scene mean? I may arrive at different conclusions in the years to come, but here is what I now believe about this hard-to-interpret moment in the Bible. The witch, like all witches, is trading in fakery.

She's engaged in a witch's sleight of hand. You know how this goes. They throw something in the fire and there is a puff of smoke. "Oh, I see your uncle. Everybody put your hands on the table." Right? Just a trick. Yet when Samuel actually appears, she's terrified! She doesn't expect a ghost, but one appears.

There is an interesting line in the Bible that adds some depth to this episode. Remember that Saul asks, "What do you see?" If we look at the notes in a King James Bible, we find the word the witch uses when she answers is *god*. The actual word is god with a small g. Literally, she says, "I see a god coming up out of the earth."[18] The word in Hebrew is *elohim*, "mighty one." She actually says, "I see a mighty being coming up out of the earth." Here's the question: Can she really summon the dead? Is it really Samuel who rises? It's very problematic.

Here's what I think happened. I think the witch was planning to fake out the unknown dude before her. She casts her spells and starts into her incantations, perhaps with all the usual paraphernalia. While all this silliness is going on, God says, "Hey, you know what I think I'll do? You want Samuel? Here's Samuel." I think God intercedes, but not to honor the witch. God forbid! She is absolutely engaged in witchcraft. Dealing with the dead is forbidden by God, and this is quite clear in Scripture. I believe God intervened in an otherwise occult process, allowing Samuel the great prophet to prophesy one last time to a fallen and doomed king.

The other possibility is that it was all witchcraft and somehow the witch was actually able to summon the dead. However, I have trouble with that. I don't believe that level of witchcraft really works. My core belief is that God intervened in the whole affair: "You want a word from Samuel? I'll give you a word from Samuel." He lets the spirit of Samuel appear. God can do that. God can transmigrate between the supernatural world and the natural world. Jesus did it. My conclusion is that God tricked the witch and Saul. "You want to deal with the dead? Here's a dead prophet. You want to know what the truth is? Here it is. You'll be dead before the sun goes down tomorrow."

The interaction between young Saul and the prophet Samuel began wonderfully with humility and grace. It ended with darkness and death and denunciation and separation and loss. Finally, on the battlefield, Saul committed suicide. His collapse cannot be seen apart from the conflict between the king and the prophet, the earthly and the divine—between the authority of Saul and the transcendent, supernatural power of God operating through the man of God.

———

Allow me to close this chapter with a personal story. When I was twenty-five, in 1972, I began pastoring my first church. An elderly man in that church told me an amazing story from his childhood. It seems his father was an elder in the local Holiness church and that church had hired a new preacher. The preacher heard that there was a moonshiner up in the hills. That Holiness preacher made the bold decision to make a house call. The elderly man, who was a little boy when this happened, said, "My father had the only Model A in the church, so he said to the preacher, 'I'll drive you.'" They drove up to the moonshiner's house, and the moonshiner came out on the front porch with a shotgun and yelled, "Get back in your car."

The elderly man remembered being a little boy sitting in the back seat of that Model A, with his dad at the wheel. When the moonshiner ordered them to leave, the preacher bravely stepped out and said, "I'm not a revenuer. I'm not from the government. I'm a pastor." The moonshiner said, "I know who you are. Get back in your car." As the preacher moved toward the man, the moonshiner stepped to him and hit him on the forehead with the heel of his hand. Having hit the pastor, he said again, "Get back in your car." The preacher stepped back and said, "Thus saith the Lord! You have tapped the man of God. And I will tap you." Then he got back in the car and they left.

About a month later, that little boy was driving with his dad, and there were people looking over a drop-off by the side of a road. His father stopped the car, told the boy to stay, and went over to see what was happening. He came back a moment later and said, "I'm going to take you to see something." He took the little boy by the hand and guided him over to the drop-off. At the bottom was the moonshiner's truck. The father said, "Come down here. You're big enough to see this, and I don't ever want you to forget it." So father and son scrambled down that hillside and pried the truck open. That moonshiner was dead. The steering column had been forced right through his forehead.

Moonshiner or monarch, the sobering truth is undimmed by the centuries. Opposing the sovereign power of God is the doorway to disaster. Saul refused to obey, and it destroyed him. He began as David began, as the chosen, God-sent, and God-ordained king. But he ended his life in witchcraft and suicidal madness. The key instrument in the clash between God and disobedient kings may well be a prophet. The violent bootlegger who dared to tap the man of God ended up dead in a ditch. The king of Israel fell on his own sword on barren Mount Gilboa. Strange isn't it? Their terrible deaths were three thousand years apart but in death they looked just the same.

LESSONS FROM OLD DR. MARK ABOUT SAMUEL

Partial obedience is disobedience.

God, through Samuel, commanded King Saul to kill all the Amalekites and all their livestock. Saul kept the best of the livestock and spared the life of the king of the Amalekites. The most pathetic part of the tragedy is that Saul actually thought he had obeyed. Saul wasn't lying just to Samuel; he was also lying to himself. This kind of self-deception is the worst of all deceptions.

Whatever the command, great leaders do what God tells them to do—everything they're told, when they're told. Leaders who deceive themselves cut corners, redefine their orders, and finally convince themselves that they really did obey.

Imagine for a moment that God told you to drive across the United States. If you drove halfway and returned, how many times would you have to make half the journey for it to equal the whole trip. Twice? What about one-fourth of the way? Four times? You cannot add up multiple episodes of partial obedience and make it equal even one moment of full obedience.

Great leaders do what they're told. They cut no corners. They refuse to offer God half measures. They never quit until the job is done. Partial obedience is disobedience.

Discern the chapters of your life.

Life is written in chapters, and one leads on to the next. To move gracefully onward and leave a chapter, even the most pleasant of chapters, and plunge into the next is actually at the heart of the science of life. Samuel had enjoyed a great season as prophet and judge. When it came time for him to stand aside and let Saul have the stage, it was hard for the old prophet, but he did it. He listened to God and moved on.

He had been a young prophet, a very young prophet and kingmaker, in his prime, but the next chapter was about being an old prophet, an absent and perhaps forgotten prophet. The last chapter was about being a judge as great as Gideon or Jephthah. In the next chapter he was to become an ex-judge, if you will, living at a mysterious and remote little school in the hills at Ramah. Also in the next chapter he was saving young David from the demonized King Saul. What if he had failed to move on?

Those who cling to one chapter or another, refusing to move on, become emotional dwarfs. Those who are afraid of the next chapter often ruin the very chapter in which they stay too long and then miss what God has for them. Great servants of God move on. They let the pages turn as God wills. He who is the author of each chapter will also, at the end of the whole book, be its finisher.

CHAPTER 5

Nathan and a Kingly Mess

But that night the word of the LORD came to Nathan, saying...
"Tell my servant David, 'This is what the LORD Almighty
says: I took you from the pasture and appointed you ruler over
my people Israel. I have been with you wherever you have gone,
and I have cut off all your enemies from before you.
Now I will make your name great.'"

—2 Samuel 7:4, 8–9

I LIKE TO COLLECT historical artifacts. One of the interesting pieces I have is a belt buckle taken from the body of a German soldier killed during the Battle of the Bulge. The buckle has a circle with a wreath on it upon which is perched an eagle with a swastika in its talons. On it are the German words *Gott mit uns*, which means "God with us." The Nazi soldier who wore that belt buckle into battle with a determination to kill Americans represented a system and a vision that was pure evil. Yet in his heart he believed that God was on his side. At least, he wore the words into battle. That belt buckle speaks clearly to the problem when politics and prophecy blend or collide.

History is replete with examples of this conflation of politics and prophecy. The extremely complex Hundred Years' War between France and England began in 1337. Its most famous battle was the Battle of Agincourt, memorialized by Shakespeare in his great play *Henry V*. The whole war was a bloody, dramatic affair, particularly the interplay between Charles VII of France and Henry VI of England.

By 1425 the war had gone so badly for France that the nation was in danger of complete subjugation. Circumstances began changing, though, when an ignorant, illiterate peasant girl claimed that she had received visions of French saints. She said the saints had told her to go to the Dauphin, the heir apparent to the French throne, and tell him that God had sent her to help the French win the war and then place him on the throne.

Strangely enough, the French were eager to believe her. There were two reasons. One was the question "What if she's right?" In other words, "What if she had indeed seen these visions and was telling the truth?" The second was that the French were losing so badly they realized if they let her do what she wanted and they continued to lose, they could blame it on her. They allowed her to do as she asked, which was to wear men's armor and lead troops. The tide of the war changed immediately. It was a truly strange episode in history. That teenaged girl named Joan, despite wearing a man's armor into battle, wouldn't carry a sword. She said she would carry a staff with a flag on it when she rode into battle, which is exactly what she did. She was eventually wounded by an arrow during one of the great battles, but there was something about her that inspired the French troops, and the tide of the war turned in France's favor.

Obviously, the visions she received, dedicated Roman Catholic that she was, were highly political, and her leadership was entirely military. Ultimately, Joan of Arc, as she came to be known, even sat in on military councils and gave advice. In time she was captured by a cadre of the French people who were favorable to the English. They sold her to the English, who charged her with many crimes, including blasphemy and cross-dressing. They convicted her as a heretic and burned her at the stake.

Later, Joan of Arc was canonized by the Roman Catholic Church. The challenge when considering Joan of Arc is this: Did she receive these visions from God? Did God even care who won the Hundred Years' War? Were her visions real? Were they manufactured? The second thing we struggle with is this: If they were real, why did the British burn her at the stake? If they weren't real, how did she get so deeply into the heart of French politics and the military? She was a teenage girl who couldn't even read. You see where I am going with this. It is always dicey when revelation, dreams, and prophecies serve political and military ends.

I can give you a more personal example from my own life. I was speaking at a college chapel some years ago, and we were facing a national election. In my talk I said that I didn't tell people how to vote and I wasn't going to endorse a candidate from the podium. I did tell them, though, that I personally would not vote for a candidate who would appoint judges to the bench willing to rule in favor of abortion. I told the audience that abortion was an important issue to me, so I had to ask myself which candidate would commit to appointing judges opposed to abortion.

Afterward, the wife of a faculty member approached me. She was absolutely furious. She said, "You used the platform of this university to deal with a political issue. That should never happen." In reply, I said, "Ma'am, I want to ask you a question. What about all the preachers in the South in the 1920s, '30s, '40s, and '50s who used that very excuse and wouldn't deal with the national sin of segregation? They hid behind that same wall you are describing. What about Dr. King when he spoke up? Was he a prophet to this nation, or was he a politician? Now, ma'am, there are times when the church must speak. What about slavery— was that a political issue? We certainly fought a highly political war over it. Was it a political issue or a spiritual issue? Can a man indeed own another man?" Oddly, the lady replied, "Well, I see your point. But abortion is different." She did not take the time to explain the distinction.

Here is the major lesson from all this: When prophets and politicians converge, it gets dangerous. It gets messy. A king is always a politician. A prophet is a voice from another world—we hope! When the two conflict over political matters, it is often ugly, disorienting, and leaves more questions than answers. When the two agree it can be worse, depending on who is agreeing with whom.

This warning about the intersection of the prophetic and the political is at the heart of the ministry of the prophet Nathan and his relationship with King David. With his appearance on the scene, everything shifts. Abraham was a prophet, as we saw, but his only real connection to kings was fighting them, fleeing them, or yielding to them. Samuel's relationship with kings is summed up by his anointing Saul, confronting Saul, and then backing away when Saul stepped away from God. Notice, he was not intimate with Saul. He also anointed David in Bethlehem and then he disappeared until David fled from Saul's presence. Then David went to Ramah, where Samuel was running a kind of Charismatic Bible college for prophets. It is important to realize that when David left that school of the prophets at Ramah, Samuel disappears from David's life. Samuel was a prophet in connection with kings but—as with Abraham—there was no intimacy.

Samuel was a prophet connected to two impressive, important kings but not in a personal relationship with either of them. There was the season, however brief, when David hid out at Ramah, but we have no account of David and Samuel's time together there. Also, I believe Samuel was a mysterious and intimidating man, a type not given to intimacy. When he died, David grieved, perhaps not so much the loss of a friend as the loss of a national iconic figure and a supernatural national resource. The lives of the prophets were by and large lonely, without intimacy between them and the kings they guided. This was especially true for several, including Moses, who had no real relationship with Pharaoh, unless you can call combat to the death a "relationship." Likewise, Abraham's only intimate connection with royalty was the stunningly intimate but fleeting and singular interaction with the mysterious Melchizedek, the king of Salem.

For King David, things change with the arrival of Nathan on the scene. Nathan is much more political. He is embroiled in all the tumult of David's house—the intrigue, the upheavals, and the conspiracies. Nathan even helps David and Bathsheba defeat an attempted coup d'état by David's son Adonijah. This is a shift, as is the fact that there are no miracles that attend Nathan's work. There's none of the supernatural, none of the unusual happenings that attended the prophetic ministry of Samuel.

Contemplate the many weird incidents in the life of Samuel. One was that after he was dead, there was the complicated matter of the witch of Endor conjuring up Samuel, or what appears to be Samuel, from the dead. Then you have the incident in which Saul and his army try repeatedly to arrest David at Ramah. They end up prophesying. Presumably, they are prophesying good about David. Finally, a frustrated Saul arrives, but he ends up pulling his clothes off, lying on the floor naked in front of David, and again, we must assume, prophesying the future king's blessing.

Nathan seems to have little of the expected prophetic personality. He's a voice of godly authority in David's life. He was tightly connected to David's court. In fact, Nathan's brother, Joel, was one of David's top military leaders. When the Bible records David's mighty ones, his *gibborim*, it also records the thirty among them who were the leaders, the best of the best, and Joel is listed.[1] That's how closely connected Nathan and his family were to the court and family of David.

Another difference is that Samuel was a prophet to a nation. He dealt with kings. He dealt with the course of the entire Hebrew nation. Nathan was a prophet, to be sure, but he was a prophet to David. As we will see, his relationship to David became ever closer as they aged. One might say he was the family priest. Some prophets were prophets "in the land." It could be said that Nathan was a prophet "in the house."

This new type of prophet with a new focus forces both the king and the prophet to reevaluate who they are. A king asks himself: "How do I balance the authority and power I have on a secular throne, in a kingdom, with a prophet who comes to me and says, 'I'm from God'?"

Read the story:

2 Samuel 7; 1 Chronicles 17.

The prophet asks, "I am a prophet of God. How does that work in the kingdoms of this world? Who am I in that tension? What is my real role? What does my proximity and access to the king mean to me? What does it mean to the king? What does it mean to the people he rules? What does it mean to me, and most important of all, what does it mean to God?"

This is the challenge for the "prophet in the house." The greater the favor God gives to religious leaders with political leaders, the greater their access to political leaders and the greater their responsibility. I have a low level of responsibility for speaking with presidents of the United States or prime ministers of England. I have never been summoned to the White House or to 10 Downing Street. Yet there are people who have a great deal of access to high-level political leaders—and not just presidents. The same principle applies: the greater the access and favor, the greater the responsibility.

We first get to know Nathan as he deals with David on the issue of the temple. David wants to build a temple for God. He speaks to Nathan and says, "I want to build a temple." At first Nathan enthusiastically affirms the idea. Later he returns to David with a revised prophecy, which on the surface feels like a rebuke. "The Lord says, 'You don't build Me a house. I'm God. I build you a house.'" Understandably, it feels like a rejection. Then Nathan says, "However, your son will build it."

God's answer is made more complete by adding the issue of blood. David was a man of war. Was he ever! God wanted a man of peace to build the temple. This must have stung a bit. David was a man of blood and warfare; from Goliath on he had been fighting the enemies of the people of God. On the other hand, God through Nathan extends two great promises of grace. One is that God will build David a house. He means, of course, not a building but a dynasty. This is a phenomenal promise. Second, God promises that though David will not build the temple, David's son will. With that David is entirely mollified and praises God elegantly for the prophetic answer.

The more salient point, however, is that this entire conversation is the context in which we meet Nathan, and it frames the nature of his entire relationship with David. Not to be passed over lightly is the fact that Nathan himself suffers a bit of a divine rebuke. It is as though God says to the prophet, "Look, check with Me first before you answer. This is important." David and Nathan are learning this prophet-king relationship thing together. Nathan's appearance in David's life is not a one-off. The issue of the temple and whether David should build it is the beginning of an incredibly complicated lifetime relationship between king and prophet, a relationship that ended only with the death of the king.

On the one hand, this is a stern reminder of God's power and prophetic authority over political and secular leaders. It is also, however, a loving and gracious reminder of God's covenantal involvement with us. God may chasten us, rebuke us, and scold us, but then turn right around and say, "However, I just want you to know how much I love you, and My covenant is still with you." Nathan played this role in David's life and made it clear that David and God had a beautiful covenant together, but there were boundaries.

Nathan is the first of a new breed of prophets, a court prophet. He is not the mysterious Samuel, who appears suddenly at propitious moments. Nor is he Moses, who comes in from the desert like the wind to confront Pharaoh and destroy his army. Nathan is more of a courtier, a palace priest if you will, a personal advisor with more than common wisdom. He was certainly a prophet, but a prophet in residence. Even more than that, he was a fixture at court. Later such court prophets, seduced by their proximity to power, became dangerous traps for subsequent kings of Israel and Judah. Nathan loved David, served him faithfully, and advised him well, but Nathan was never a compromised sycophant.

Nathan doesn't appear in the story of David relative to the temple because he swoops in with a divine directive. He is summoned. David calls him in to announce and get God's approval for his plan to build a temple. That must have been an extraordinary moment for David's household prophet and, unfortunately, Nathan made a false start. The plan sounded so good that instead of waiting to hear from God, Nathan answers spontaneously. Only later, after hearing from God, did Nathan go back to the king with a prophetic answer.

Evidently Nathan learned from his first false start. His ability to hear from God and his courageous willingness to tell King David what he heard prepared Nathan for the great defining moment of his life. After three thousand years, Nathan's voice still thunders four words that made him eternally famous and changed the heart of a king: "Thou art the man."[2]

Following his interaction with David concerning the temple, the next and far more dramatic entrance of Nathan is over the matter of Bathsheba. This time he was not summoned by David. His easy access to the king is indicative of their close relationship. Nathan appears before King David with the story of a rich man who steals and devours the pet lamb of a poor man. Nathan's story is now so famous that it may seem less than remarkable to the modern hearer, but it was a brilliant allegory filled with pathos and was well designed to stir David's sense of justice. It also served perfectly to bait the prophet's trap.

David's howl of outrage over the stolen lamb and his judgment that the perpetrator deserved to die for the crime was exactly what Nathan had hoped for. Pointing his finger at his king's face, the palace prophet proved that he was no compromised pretender to the role of prophet. "Thou art the man!"

Read the story:

2 Samuel 12:1–15.

The moment is dramatic and pregnant with implications. Nathan's courage in that moment is easily underestimated. Much is made of David's celebrated response, of his brokenhearted repentance and subsequent renewal. Indeed, much should be made of it. I wrote about this extensively in my book *David the Great*. Having said that, Nathan's incredible prophetic courage may sometimes be overlooked.

His words are not the friendly advice of an in-house prophet announcing God's decision as to whom He has chosen to build the temple. This scene is far more reminiscent of John the Baptist railing against the incestuous adultery of King Herod. Unlike Herod and the Baptist, the intimate relationship between David and Nathan complicates the scene to no end; I strongly suspect that it is much more difficult for a "prophet in residence" to publicly denounce his friend and patron king. It certainly took courage. David could easily have ordered that Nathan be executed on the spot. While David's brokenness is salutary, Nathan's courage is remarkable.

But this is not the end of the scene. First, Nathan exposes

David's compound sins of adultery, conspiracy, and murder. This alone might have been a suicide mission for Nathan. Then, when David admits to the sin, God sends Nathan to announce the dreadful punishment. The baby conceived in adultery must die and David's family will be filled with division. This must have been an unpleasant duty for Nathan. Who wouldn't prefer to announce God's grace and reconciliation rather than judgment, death, and grief— and perhaps worst of all, a lifetime of familial turmoil?

Consider what God is asking Nathan to say to David. "The baby is going to die. You are going to spend the rest of your life with enemies coming after you. In addition, your family is going to be filled with rebellion, and somebody is going to use your wives in broad daylight." Before you say such things to a king, you'd better have heard from God. Obviously, Nathan had heard from God. Everything he speaks is fulfilled. Every one of those prophecies comes true. The king's destiny is sealed. David fights, prays, and calls out to God, but the baby dies. There's nothing David can do about that. Furthermore, there is no peace for David inside his family—for the rest of his life.

David's life is filled with warfare, just as Nathan predicted, and his family is filled with rebellion. There are two major coups d'état led by his sons Absalom and Adonijah. Then, when Absalom takes Jerusalem and drives David out, ten concubines are left behind to take care of the palace. In his fierce hatred for his father, Absalom sets up a tent on the roof of the palace and methodically rapes them. Thus, that awful prophecy is fulfilled.

There is an important lesson in this for us. Everybody wants to prophesy happy times—blessing, prosperity, joy, and goodness. It takes a serious and seasoned prophet to say, "I know what you've done. The baby will die. You're going to have a lifetime of warfare and bloodshed. Your family will be filled with rebellion. Moreover, somebody's going to rape your wives in broad daylight because you took a man's life and bride." Only a prophet can declare such a message, only a man of God who has heard from God. No fear of the king can dissuade him from speaking truth.

David confesses. He repents. Soon after, Bathsheba conceives another child, whom they name Solomon. And Nathan says, "This child will rule in your place."[3] So the prophecy of punishment and hardship and the baby who dies is replaced by a baby who lives. The child of guilt and death is replaced by the child of grace. What made the difference? A repentant king, to be sure, but the catalytic power was a fearless prophet who revealed and rebuked the secret sins of a king.

Many years ago I was speaking at an international Bible school for the Pentecostal Holiness denomination in London. There were students from all over the world but almost no British students. I had lectured all day, and then had dinner with them. Just before I left, they asked if I would pray with them. There were perhaps twenty or twenty-five students in the room at that time.

I went around the room, laying my hands on them and praying for each of them. Finally, I came to one boy about whom I knew nothing whatsoever. When I laid hands on him, a pain shot through me—literal, physical pain. I strongly sensed the Lord speaking in my heart to say, "I have prepared you here to go back to your country and lay down your life." The older you get, the younger everybody else looks. This young man looked to me like he was about twelve years old. I remember thinking, "God, I don't want to say those words to this boy." In answer, God said, "If I can't trust you with the whole message, why would I give you any at all?"

So I laid my hands on the young man, and I began crying. I said, "Son, anybody can miss God, and I can miss God more than many, but I'm going to tell you what I heard." I then told him what the Lord had spoken to me. When I did, the teachers and all the students started praising God, loudly and enthusiastically. It confused me. I said, "I'm not sure you heard what I said."

The president of the Bible school came up to me and said, "We heard what you said, Dr. Rutland. The reason we are praising God is this: last week God revealed in a prophetic service that this boy would go back to his country and give his life. Today, when you spoke, it was a witness of the presence of God. We're not cheering in praise of God because he's going to die. We're cheering in praise of God because the word of God is confirmed." I said to the boy, "How do you feel about this?" He said, "All these other students came here to learn how to live. I came here to learn how to die."

I'll never forget that moment. It confirms to me that the ministry of the prophet—and I do not consider myself to be one—has to be filled with tears and fears or it would not be real. The closer the access to the throne, the greater the challenge and the greater the risk.

At this point in David's story Nathan disappears for a few years. We're going to let him go, but he will come back.

In the meantime, another prophet arises. His name is Gad. In the Bible, Gad is called both a prophet and a seer. He is like Samuel, who started out being called a seer, but the Bible ceases referring to him by that name and transitions to calling him a prophet. Gad is a seer. The word *seer* means exactly what it sounds like: a seer is a person who sees things by the power of the Spirit.

We have an example of this when Saul first encounters Samuel. Saul is chasing his father's lost donkeys and has been looking everywhere for them. Finally someone says, "There is a seer over here, and we'll go over and ask him, and see if he can see."[4]

Now, there are false seers, witchcraft seers, who see into a crystal ball or tea leaves or something of that nature. That's false and it's witchcraft. Samuel is a man of God who is a seer, so when Saul finds Samuel, he asks that Samuel would see where the donkeys are. The Lord shows Samuel, but beyond that he sees that Saul will be the next king. Samuel tells Saul, "Go home. Your father's donkeys have returned. Your father is not worried about the donkeys anymore. He's worried about you. Go home." Therefore Samuel appears first as a seer.

Gad is called a seer more often than Samuel. In the Talmud, the rabbinical writings about the Old Testament, the authors give Gad credit for writing a lost book about David. They also believe that Gad wrote part of the books of Samuel. We don't know that from Scripture, of course, but this shows how much esteem the rabbis had for Gad.

Gad's initial appearance in David's life is hardly more than a cameo and gives no indication of how significant a role he will play later on. This first interaction between

David and Gad the seer is a warning. During David's exile and flight from his father-in-law, King Saul, Gad suddenly appeared with the warning not to stay where he was, that it was not the safe stronghold David thought it was.

This simple yet life-saving message was the extent of Gad's first appearance. "Do not stay in the stronghold. Go into the land of Judah."[5] Simple but gripping enough, and it must have borne the full weight of prophetic authority, for on the basis of that brief message alone David flees to the Forest of Hereth. In other words, Gad's first words to David saved David's life. When Gad shows up again, he is a proven commodity, a prophet with authority and a messenger to be trusted. And David did indeed trust him.

The second time Gad appears is more typical of Nathan's style. David, if you remember, wanted to take a census.[6] Israel was forbidden to take a census because the weight of numbers might appeal to the narcissistic pride of the king. Joab, David's general, tells David, "Don't take the census," but David does it anyway. Gad then comes to David and declares a very unusual message. "God's going to punish you. That's done. There's nothing you can do about that. You took the census, and God's going to punish you. But there are three choices. You can have years of disease, or you can fall to your enemies, or you can have famine." David replies, "I won't choose. I will only tell you what I don't want. Don't let me fall into the hands of men. God is a God of mercy, so I'll let God decide." So God then sends a pestilence on Israel, and seventy thousand people die.

The grief and devastation of such a sudden pestilence would have been a national heartache. Seventy thousand deaths! Think of it. David's sin with Bathsheba cost two lives. David's sin in the matter of the census cost seventy thousand. David is horrified, of course, and cries out to the Lord. "Kill me," David says. "These people didn't do anything. Kill me." Instead, God lifts the pestilence and sends the prophet Gad with a new message. This third visit is different from either of the first two and is, by any estimation, the most consequential. The result of Gad's third appearance is still at the very center of geopolitical and religious conflict in the Middle East today.

Gad's message is that David should buy the stone threshing floor of a Jebusite man named Araunah, or Ornan. At Gad's instruction David buys the massive stone and offers a sacrifice there, but that is hardly the end of the story. It is over that huge stone that Solomon builds the temple. It is over that same stone that the Dome of the Rock stands today.

It is impossible to overstate the biblical and historical consequence of that one prophetic instruction. Each of Gad's three prophetic appearances in David's life were powerful with serious implications for David and for his people. The first, at the stronghold, saved David's life. The second announced the judgment of God, which meant the deaths of tens of thousands. The third brought healing and grace and an end to the pestilence. Beyond any argument, Gad's third prophetic utterance is his greatest of all. Gad may be a little-known prophet to many today, but it was through his prophecy that King David purchased what has become the most important rock on the most important mountain in the most important country in the world.

Despite Gad's importance in David's life, it is still Nathan, the aging palace prophet, who is there at the end. Like the

Ghost of Christmas Past in Charles Dickens' *A Christmas Carol*, with King David horribly sick, Nathan suddenly reappears. He arrives in the nick of time to thwart a coup attempt engineered by Joab. The plot was designed to put Adonijah on the throne instead of Solomon.

With the help of Bathsheba and others, Nathan runs a countercoup like a seasoned politician, and Solomon is anointed king as God intended. It is interesting to note that while Nathan was indisputably a prophet, at the end of his ministry the old prophet turned out to be equally adept at palace intrigue.

LESSONS FROM OLD DR. MARK ABOUT NATHAN

Beware of the seduction of power.

The purpose of the prophet is not to please kings. From time to time God may grant a "prophet" (a spiritual person) access to a secular leader, a politician, or an oligarch, and that access may become great favor. Such a moment is a gift, not to the prophet but to the secular leader. It is a dangerous moment for the prophet, a high-risk assignment that will require courage, discernment, wisdom, and self-control. The secular leader needs that prophet. He needs the voice of God in his ear. He especially needs the stern rebuke, the firm confrontation, and the call to truth and repentance. The prophet does not need the leader, but the attendant favor and access can be seductive. The atmosphere is toxic around the leaders of this present age, especially for prophets.

If God should ever grant you favor and access to some famous, wealthy person, use it for God's glory and for that person's good. But when you sit down at the table of power, hold a knife to your own throat.

Do not put words in God's mouth.

Some in the Christian world, sadly even those who are prominent leaders, have become cavalier about saying, "Thus saith the Lord." When their "prophecies" turn out to be false or at best unfulfilled, they just leave them behind, ignore what they have said, and brush away their tracks with a leafy bough. Or worst of all, they accuse those who would hold them accountable of being legalistic and judgmental. To err is human, yet that proverb is not a license to use the name of the Lord in vain.

In America we recently had a rash of unfulfilled political "prophecies." Many of those whose so-called prophecies turned out to be false never really dealt with their errors publicly. One man did not sweep his failed prophecy under the rug. Instead, he owned it, humbly apologized for it, and vowed to search his soul for how he could get it so wrong. That is more or less what Nathan had to do when David told him he wanted to build a temple for God. At first Nathan enthusiastically affirmed David's idea. After hearing from God, Nathan had to reverse himself. That must not have been easy, but he did it. He humbled himself before God and the king and told David, "Do not build the temple. That is reserved for another."

The lesson is simple. Do not put words in God's mouth. Say only what you have heard from Him—nothing added and nothing shaved off. Just say what you heard from God. A "word of prophecy" is not a Christian parlor game. If you get it wrong, do what Nathan did and ad-mit it. Humble yourself, apologize, and commit yourself to listening better, speaking less, and being held accountable.

CHAPTER 6

Four Kings, Six Prophets, and a God on the Move

Ahijah the prophet of Shiloh…took hold of the new cloak…and tore it into twelve pieces. Then he said to Jeroboam, "Take ten pieces for yourself, for this is what the LORD, the God of Israel, says: 'See, I am going to tear the kingdom out of Solomon's hand and give you ten tribes. But for the sake of my servant David and the city of Jerusalem, which I have chosen out of all the tribes of Israel, he will have one tribe.'"

—1 Kings 11:29–32

ISTORY AND NAMES can often be confusing. Perhaps, like many others, you struggled in school with sorting out the names of American presidents. I think many students have a hard time with the difference, for example, between Teddy Roosevelt, who pronounced his name "Roos-a-velt," and Franklin Delano Roosevelt, who pronounced his name "Rose-a-velt." Then there was John Adams and his relationship to John Quincy Adams, and George H. W. Bush to George W. Bush. Such things can be confusing to a student.

A similar challenge is presented by the kings and prophets of the Old Testament. Israel's united monarchy split into two nations, Judah and Israel. Judah is really the heart of old Israel—but it's not called Israel. It's called Judah. The breakaway portion of Israel calls itself Israel, yet it's not centered around Jerusalem and it's not Judah. It's the northern kingdom.

So after the reigns of Saul, David, and Solomon, many kings in these two different kingdoms have the same or similar names. Furthermore, you have a number of prophets. Some speak to the kings of Israel and some deal with the kings of Judah. Some even minister back and forth between both Israel and Judah. Making it worse, some of the prophets have similar names and—God help us!—some of the prophets have the same names as some of the kings.

If you find all this confusing, you are not alone. Generations of Bible readers have struggled to keep it straight.

131

In this chapter, I want to deal with four kings and six prophets. Given that I'll be talking about ten different people, it's important for us to keep their names straight. Until the end of Solomon's reign, Israel is simply called Israel. That's hardly confusing. Then, after Solomon's reign, there is a split. As I explained above, the northern part of Israel breaks off from the southern part. That northern part is called Israel, the southern part is called Judah. So far, so good!

Here are the four kings. The first is Jeroboam, the king of the northern kingdom of Israel. Jeroboam led the people back into worshipping golden calves. The second is Asa, the good king of Judah. Jehoshaphat, king of Judah, is also a good king. Ahab, one of the worst of all the kings of Israel, is the fourth.

These kings interact with six different prophets. Another name for this chapter could be "The Tomb of the Unknown Prophet" because some of the prophets we are about to examine will be unknown to you. In fact, hardly anybody knows about them. By the time we are done here, you will know why. The names of these six prophets are Ahijah, Iddo, Jehu, Azariah, Jahaziel, and Micaiah. I know this sounds like the partners in a Tel Aviv law firm, but they are actually the names of some pretty powerful prophets of God.

The first of these six prophets is Ahijah. He lived at the end of the reign of Solomon and the beginning of the time of Jeroboam—which is a long time. Solomon had fallen into sin at the end of his reign, during the same years that a young general named Jeroboam arose. One day, as Jeroboam returned from a great battle, he was met in the field by Ahijah the prophet. The two men faced each other, and Ahijah did an unusual thing. He took a new cloak and, with Jeroboam looking on, chopped it into twelve pieces. As he set two of the pieces aside, he said, "Those represent Judah and Benjamin. God will keep those to the house of David because He loved David. Even though Solomon has fallen into sin, those two will stay in the house of David. The rest, these ten here, represent the other ten tribes." Then Ahijah stacked up the ten pieces of cloth and gave them to Jeroboam.

Jeroboam is thus predicted to become the first king of the northern kingdom. He became Solomon's sworn enemy. In fact, it is when Solomon tries to have Jeroboam killed that the young general leads the ten tribes in breaking away and forming that northern kingdom of Israel.

Notice that the practice of prophets anointing kings is consistent and important throughout the Old Testament. Samuel anointed Saul, just as he later anointed David. Then Solomon was anointed by the prophet Nathan. You may remember that as David lay dying, there was a coup

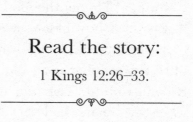

Read the story:

1 Kings 12:26–33.

d'état led by Adonijah. David rose up on his deathbed, had Nathan anoint Solomon, and thus Solomon became the true king. Likewise, Ahijah anoints Jeroboam as king of a new Israel. Here's the principle: the reign of kings often begins with declaration and anointing by the prophets of God, but that does not always determine the outcome.

Soon Jeroboam begins to fear that his people will be pulled away from him by the lure of Jerusalem, especially the temple, and drift back into Judah. It is not hard to imagine. Jerusalem was the capital of the old country. It is the hub, the center. The temple is there. The base of Judaic thought is there. Everything from religion to politics is centered in Jerusalem. Everyone knows God's hand is on Jerusalem.

Jeroboam wants to cut those religious and cultural ties. To do that he builds a new temple at Bethel and erects a new altar. He has no authority to do this. In fact, it's blasphemous. Furthermore, in his desire to fashion something new, he sets up golden calves—thus harkening back to a motif that dates to the bondages we see in the Book of Exodus. Remember the worship of the golden calf that Aaron built? Jeroboam is resurrecting it, and claiming, "This is the God that brought you out of Egypt. It was not Jehovah; it was actually this golden calf."

Read the story:

1 Kings 14:1–18.

Because of this, Ahijah disappears from Jeroboam's life until the prophet is an old, old man. During this time, he becomes blind. The two men are brought back together when Jeroboam's little boy, who is named Abijah, becomes sick. Jeroboam thinks he's dying and tells his wife, "Go to Shiloh, where the old prophet is, and disguise yourself, and tell the prophet, 'I've got a sick child. Will he live or die?' And he'll tell us whether the child will live or die, but he won't know who you are."

Now, isn't this a remarkable thing? The prophet is so old that he's now blind. Yet Jeroboam tells his wife to disguise herself. It is almost humorous, isn't it? Why would you wear a disguise to visit a blind man? Obviously, Jeroboam is so confused spiritually that he thinks this old prophet, who can see through the veil of space and time and see the future, can't see through a disguise.

Still, Jeroboam was right to fear Ahijah's prophetic gifts, because before his wife even arrives at her destination, God speaks to Ahijah and says, "Jeroboam's wife is on her way to see you to ask about her child. Tell her the boy will die. And rebuke her, and send a message to Jeroboam." When the woman steps into Ahijah's house, the moment her footsteps make a sound, the old blind man says, "I know you're the wife of Jeroboam. Come in." We can only imagine this very scary moment. The woman has gone all the way there to fool the old guy with a disguise, and the minute he hears her footsteps, he says, "You're the wife of Jeroboam. Come in."

———

Ahijah tells Jeroboam's wife two things. The first is that her child will die. "When I heard your footsteps, I knew who you were. When your footsteps enter the city, the child will die." In essence he is saying, "You, by your behavior, have killed the child. When you go back home, the child will die." And then he says, "Take this message to Jeroboam: Israel will be taken captive. The people of Israel, the northern kingdom, will be taken beyond the river."

The message to the king is that he and his people were going to be captured and the ten tribes taken away. That prophecy was not fulfilled for two hundred years, but when it was fulfilled, it was a nightmare.

It is unsettling but true: there is no time limit on true

prophecy. Once God reveals something, it unfolds in eternal time, not earthly time. God can see through to the future, He can see through any disguise, He can see the reality of a thing, and the future is as the past to God Almighty. Ahijah's prophecy takes two hundred years to be fulfilled as men reckon time, but it's the snap of a finger to God.

As to the second prophet of the six, oddly enough, no one is sure of his name. It may be Iddo. That's the name used for this man in several places in the Talmud, but remember the Talmud is not the Old Testament. It's a book in which famous rabbis have written commentaries about the Old Testament. They are very important in Judaic history and culture, but they're not Scripture. Still, sometimes it's helpful to know what the Talmud says, and the Talmud tells us that this unknown prophet is a man named Iddo. I'll go with that assumption.

Iddo is also called a "man of God." In Hebrew, this is *Ish Elohim*. *Ish* means "a man, a person"—it's what Adam called himself at the very beginning. *Ish* is Adam and *Isha* is Eve. So *Ish Elohim* is a "man of God." The word *nabi* means "prophet." It's interesting that this man is a prophet, a *nabi*, but he is more commonly referred to in Scripture as the "man of God." This tells us a great deal about his character and the power of his prophetic gifts.

When Iddo goes to see Jeroboam, the stories begin to interweave. Ahijah has already prophesied to Jeroboam: "Take the northern ten tribes and start a nation; you'll be the king." Jeroboam then builds his idolatrous altar. Afterward,

Ahijah disappears from Jeroboam's life and goes to Shiloh. The wife of Jeroboam then goes to Shiloh to receive the prophecy that her child will die. Between these two events Iddo arrives at Jeroboam's headquarters. He prophesies but his prophecy is unique in one way: He does not address Jeroboam. He addresses the altar.

I've actually seen this altar. Archaeologists discovered it in the north of Israel in the region of Dan. My son, Travis, and I went there together. As we walked on one of the false altars mentioned in Scripture, we discussed the downfall of nations and the devastation of idolatry. I will never forget that conversation. Picture this scene. The prophet approaches the huge, idolatrous altar erected by Jeroboam. There are people worshipping around this altar, offering sacrifices to their false god. As they do, Iddo walks up, raises his hands, and speaks to the altar. He says, "Oh, altar. Oh, altar." Then he prophesies. "A man will be born in the house of David. His name will be Josiah. [Remember this is three hundred years before Josiah was born.] And altar, he will tear you down and burn bones on you."[1]

As you can imagine, Jeroboam is furious. He points at Iddo and commands, "Seize him!" Instantly, Jeroboam's arm becomes like wood. The literal Hebrew words declare that his hand "dried up." It is frozen. In fact, his hand dries up so thoroughly that he cannot withdraw it.

It's a serious thing to tamper with a real prophet of God.

Jeroboam is now in an awkward position. Why? There is only one person who can heal his frozen arm, and that is the prophet he just ordered to be seized! Realizing this, Jeroboam begs the man of God to restore his hand. Here is the astonishing thing: Iddo prays for Jeroboam and heals him. Amazing! Iddo prays for the rebellious king and heals him. It's a complicated story. First, the prophecy was never against Jeroboam personally. It was against the altar. Second, even in the midst of prophetic confrontation there is healing grace.

When God's judgment is coming on something or someone, don't get in the way. In this case, the judgment pronounced was on the altar. Think about what the prophet said. "Someone named Josiah from the household of David will come and tear you down, and you will rupture and break open, and the ash will pour out. And someone from the household of David will come and tear you down and burn bones on you." All Jeroboam had to do was wait. Instead, he points at the prophet and orders him to be seized. As he does, his arm withers, the altar cracks, and all the ash from the sacrificial animals pours out, validating the prophecy. It is then that Jeroboam says, "Please pray for me," and Iddo prays for him and he's healed. Yet Jeroboam would never have needed healing if he had not gotten in the way of God's judgment.

This story then gets even more complicated. God has told this man of God, this *ish Elohim*, not to stay in Israel. "Go back to Judah. Go back to Shiloh. Get out of there. Don't eat there; don't stay there; don't rest there; don't let anybody give you hospitality." In other words, "Stay away from the seductive power of the north. Declare the message I've given you, and get out of there." King Jeroboam, when his hand is healed, says, "I'll give you anything—half my kingdom, anything you want—but stay with me." The man of God says what he's supposed to say: "I won't take anything from you, and I won't eat a morsel of your food." He then starts traveling home.

On the way, another man comes out to meet the prophet, and the Bible calls him an "old prophet." Notice that no king is involved in this part of the story. What happens next is prophet to prophet—and both of the prophets are unnamed. The old prophet says, "Come and stay with me, visit with me, eat with me. I heard what you did. Come and stay at my house." The *ish Elohim*, the younger prophet who may be named Iddo, says, "No. I can't do that. God told me not to stay here." The older prophet says, "The angel of the Lord came to me and told me to tell you it was all right."

Iddo goes and eats at the older prophet's house. While they're eating, the older prophet suddenly has the spirit of conviction come upon him, and he blurts out, "I lied to you." Even worse, the older prophet says, "I lied to you. I did not see the angel of the Lord. I just wanted you in my house. Now you're going to die."

If you have trouble with this story, you are not alone. This is one of the more troubling stories in the Bible. After Iddo eats, he mounts his donkey and starts for home. Soon after, a lion attacks and kills him. Someone runs to the old prophet and says, "A lion has mauled and killed a man, and he's lying in the road." This surviving prophet responds, "Oh yeah, that's Iddo. I tricked him, and God killed him." The old prophet then goes out to where all this occurred. He finds three things: Iddo's body, the lion, and Iddo's donkey. The lion is apparently standing guard over the body and the donkey. The older prophet then loads Iddo's body on the donkey and takes him home.

John Wesley's commentary on this passage reveals the

differences in perspective that can exist between generations.[2] Remember that Wesley lived in the 1700s. The remarkable thing in the story for Wesley was something we likely wouldn't even think of. He said, "What a miracle! The lion didn't eat the donkey." What most stood out to him was that under normal circumstances the lion would eat the donkey. Frankly, I had hardly even thought of this. Yet for Wesley, the most remarkable fact was that *the lion didn't eat the donkey because the old prophet needed the donkey to get the body home.* Such a practical application was wasted on me, a child of my own century. That God kept the donkey alive to carry the corpse seemed a trivial miracle to me, living in an age of easily rented trucks.

The story does not even end there. The old prophet had a tomb, and he decided to put Iddo in it. He then gave instructions: "When I die, bury me next to him in my tomb."

Now, I can't pretend to understand all that God intends from this story, but a few things seem obvious. First, when God speaks to you, don't be intimidated by someone else's pretended spirituality. When you've heard from God, nobody has the spiritual authority to move you from the safety and certainty of God's will.

Second, be suspicious of anybody who claims to have seen the angel of the Lord. I'm not saying this never happens, but I can echo the Bible: *Test every spirit.* This is important. I'm sorry to say that I know people who claim to see angels popping out of the woodwork. Keep in mind that angelic appearances are rare—so rare that they are noteworthy even in the Bible. I certainly believe in angelic appearances, but anytime somebody tells me he's had coffee with angels that morning, I just steward a healthy skepticism. I am not convinced by the words alone. "The angel of the Lord told me!" is easily said. Be careful, be wise, and be discerning.

Third, if someone tells you that an angel of the Lord has said something contrary to either what God has told you or, more importantly, Scripture, get out of there. Let me say it again, *get out of there!* Nothing good will come of staying around a person who is so deceived.

Finally, keep in mind one of the main lessons of this book: people who have spiritual revelations, who may be prophets, are not made perfect by those revelations. Elijah was a prophet who struggled with depression and fear. Iddo was a prophet who died because

Read the story:

1 Kings 16:1–7.

of a stupid act of disobedience. These mistakes and follies didn't invalidate the prophetic authority in these men's lives, but their anointing didn't protect them from the consequences of their actions.

As is perhaps fitting for such an unusual story, its epilogue does not occur for three hundred years. It comes through the third prophet, named Jehu, not to be confused with the very bloodthirsty king named Jehu.

Jehu's father was a lesser-known prophet named Hanani, who had confronted Asa, the king of Judah, regarding his alliance with Ben-Hadad, a pagan king of Syria. Though Asa was one of the good kings of Judah, he had made an alliance with the Syrians to attack Israel, the northern kingdom. Hanani rebuked Asa and said, "Why are you hooked up with these pagans?"

Interestingly, Jehu rebuked Baasha, king of Israel, in the same way because he murdered Jeroboam's son and all his family. In fact, Baasha wiped out the king's entire household. Jehu also rebuked Jehoshaphat, a good king of Judah, for helping Ahab, an evil king of Israel. He asked the same question his father had asked of Asa: "Why are you hooked up with this evil guy?"

I find this intriguing. Father and son both shared a prophetic ministry, both had the authority and the power to speak to kings, and both rebuked them for the same thing. "Why are you with Ben-Hadad, this Syrian? Why are you with Ahab, this evil king of Israel?" The son became more famous and more prominent than the father, but their ministries were similar.

The question asked by both prophets was the same. Shall you help the ungodly? They were not urging leaders to be merciless to the lost. Instead, they were challenging those who formed alliances with ungodly leaders. Partnerships are difficult on their best day. Partnerships with people who are not following God are downright dangerous. This was the basis of the rebuke to both kings: Be careful of forming professional leadership relationships with people who are not as committed to God as you are. The New Testament says the same thing. "Do not be unequally yoked."[3] Of course, the reference is to marriage, but the same truth is transferable to business and ministry. Don't go into business partnerships and leadership covenants with those whose lives and ethics are not committed to God. It never ends well.

The fourth prophet I want to deal with is Jahaziel, who first appears when he gives a positive word for King Jehoshaphat. It is a moment when the Moabites, the Ammonites, and others have formed an alliance of enemy armies and are attacking Judah. Jehoshaphat is a good and righteous king of Judah. Faced with this overwhelming invasion, Jehoshaphat calls a prayer meeting. He says, "Let's worship the Lord, and let's pray, and let's seek God. We cannot possibly defeat this massive army on our own."

It is at this moment that Jahaziel suddenly appears. Oddly, we don't know where he came from, we don't know anything about him except for a few names in his genealogical line, and he never appears again. Yet he is an important prophet because he encourages Jehoshaphat. He says, "You're doing the right thing! You're doing exactly the right thing."

This is important. We tend to think of all prophets as being only like Nathan:

Read the story:

2 Chronicles 20:1–29.

"Thou art the man." Or Ahijah confronting Jeroboam. We think of them as confrontational, angry, and harsh. Yet a prophet can have a positive message of affirmation, and they often do in Scripture. Jahaziel shows us this side of the prophetic. He says, "You're doing the right thing. Be courageous. God will win this supernaturally. And there's power in worship."

I spent twenty years in the United Methodist Church. Sadly, that church is now fracturing and sinking. A once-great revival movement is now a train wreck in slow motion, largely because many years ago the leadership lurched hard to the left socially, theologically, and spiritually.

I served in the United Methodist Church for two decades. In 1975, Alison and I received the baptism of the Holy Spirit. This was obviously life-changing and redirected everything about our ministry. In 1977, I resigned from my Methodist church and launched a Methodist evangelistic ministry, preaching the full gospel from church to church. I wanted to preach the message of Pentecost to Methodists. I prayed that God would somehow use me to bring revival in the Methodist church.

Let me tell you that Alison and I lived for the next thirteen years, from 1975 until 1988, in constant battle. I was hauled before the bishop for preaching error. In that very difficult meeting the bishop demanded, "What are you preaching?" I said, "Sir, I'm not preaching one thing that John Wesley didn't preach." I'll never forget what he said to me: "John Wesley couldn't be ordained in the Methodist church today." I said, "Well, I stand with Wesley."

He pressed me further. "What are you preaching? What part of Wesley are you preaching?" I answered as clearly as I knew how, "I preach salvation through the blood of Jesus and sanctifying power through the Holy Spirit." He said, "Are you talking about old second blessing holiness?" I said, "Bishop, that is certainly one way to say it."

It is important for you to absorb what happened next. The bishop turned to one of the district superintendents in the room and said, "Did you know anybody still believed that?" I said, "Well, I do." I tell this story to speak to the vast chasm between what God had done in my life and what was happening in the leadership of the Methodist

Church. This battle was constant and lasted more than a decade. I was hauled before the bishop five times. Finally, the Methodist church was going to co-opt my ministry, which was called Global Servants. They informed me that they were going to pass a rule at the North Georgia Conference that any Methodist preacher who led a 501(c) (3) nonprofit organization should know that the Methodist Church had the right to appoint the majority of that organization's board members. This meant, essentially, a takeover. I argued. I pleaded. They were adamant. "We're going to do it." I said, "I can't believe you're going to do this. You're literally going to force me to leave the Methodist Church. I'll leave, but I have to ask, Why would you want me to leave?" They said, "We're going to pass the rule. You don't have to leave. All you have to do is let us appoint the board members to your ministry."

Finally, they scheduled a vote to occur at the annual conference in Augusta, Georgia. On the night before the vote, I was in my hotel room, pacing back and forth. I was trying to decide what to do. Should I get a lawyer? Should I resign? I was so young and so confused. I called my wife and I said, "This thing's going to be horrible tomorrow. It's awful." I was so upset. I didn't want to go to court against the church, but I couldn't believe the actions they were planning against me and other ministers like me.

Suddenly, there was a knock on my hotel room door. When I opened the door, there was a man standing there. I had never seen him before, nor have I seen him since. He said, "Are you Mark Rutland?" I said, "I am." He said, "This is not your battle. This is the Lord's. Be at peace." With that he turned and walked away. I said to him, "Wait a minute!" But he was gone. He had already walked to the end of the hallway and out an exit door. Suddenly, tremendous peace came over me.

The next morning when I parked my car and started across the parking lot toward the meeting, the district superintendent who had been fighting me for years approached. He said, "OK, OK, it's off."

I decided not to let him off the hook. I said, "What do you mean it's off? What's off?"

"Oh, you know what I mean."

"No, sir, I don't. What do you mean it's off?"

He said, "We're not going to vote on that."

I said, "Not going to vote on what?"

"OK, OK, OK. I know you're enjoying this. We're not going to vote on that resolution."

I said, "That resolution about you appointing board members to my organization? You're not going to vote on that?"

"No," he said, "We're not going to vote. That's off, that's off."

I said, "Are you telling me you're not going to vote this morning and that if I leave, you'll vote on it? What are you telling me?"

He said, "We will never, ever vote on that resolution." He turned around and started to walk away.

I said, "Can you tell me why?"

He said, "I can, but I won't." And he kept walking.

I found out later that another Methodist preacher, who I didn't know at the time, also had a 501(c)(3) organization, and his attorney called the district superintendent and said, "If you pass that resolution, I'll sue you and I'll see you in court." I don't know anything about that man or his lawyer. Here's what I do know: it wasn't my fight, just as the visitor to my hotel room had said.

I'm reminded of this episode in my life because the counsel of that man at my hotel room door is very much what Jahaziel said to Jehoshaphat: "This is not your fight." Sometimes the word of prophecy comes just to encourage and confirm. There is no rebuke. There is no direction. There is just confirmation and affirmation. Our job is simply to stand and wait upon the hand of God.

Now, a fifth prophet I want to deal with was named Azariah. He is listed as the son of Oded. Azariah meets King Asa of Judah on the way home from a truly stunning military victory. An Ethiopian army of a million troops had marched north out of Ethiopia, through Egypt, and into Israel. Yet as powerful as that Ethiopian

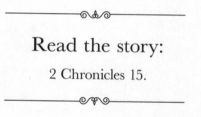

Read the story:

2 Chronicles 15.

army was, Asa and his forces defeated them. During King Asa's return from this battle, Azariah approaches him and, as with Jahaziel to Jehoshaphat, he speaks a word of encouragement. Yet it's encouragement with an edge. Azariah says to King Asa, "The point here is not the victory. Yes, you've had a victory. Yes, God gave you the victory. Yes, we rejoice in it. But the point is that you lead righteously after the victory." This is important. Clearly, Azariah's prophetic relationship to Asa was about his character and the nature of his leadership, not simply about his success.

We come then to our sixth prophet, but in order to understand his significance we have to know the importance of two kings: Ahab and Jehoshaphat. Remember that Ahab is a wicked king and he's married to one of the most evil figures in the Bible—Jezebel. Together, Ahab and Jezebel rule Israel, the northern kingdom, while, of course, Jehoshaphat rules Judah in the south.

━━━━━━ ❧ ━━━━━━

Read the story:

1 Kings 22.

━━━━━━ ❧ ━━━━━━

Ahab sends a message to Jehoshaphat in which he says, "Ramoth Gilead belongs to me, and the Syrians have taken it, and I want to get it back. Come and fight with me, and let's be one army." Ramoth Gilead was a city on the other side of the Jordan. Jehoshaphat replies, "My troops shall be like your troops; my army will be like your army."

Something must have nagged at Jehoshaphat's mind as he and the wicked king Ahab headed to the battlefield because Jehoshaphat asks, "Are there any prophets? Let's get some prophets to prophesy over this battle." Ahab replies, "Oh yeah. We've got a lot of prophets." Ahab assembles his usual crowd of favorable prophets and all of them, including the "lead" false prophet Zedekiah, begin saying, "Oh, you're going to win. This is great. Everything's going great, so go get them. You are absolutely going to win."

Clearly, Jehoshaphat is concerned by this. He asks, "Is there a prophet of the Lord?" Ahab answers, "OK. There is one guy. But I hate him because he never has anything good to say to me. His name is Micaiah." Wisely, Jehoshaphat says, "Let's get him. Let's see what he has to say."

So they send somebody to get Micaiah. While they await

Micaiah's arrival, Zedekiah attempts a flamboyant prophetic statement. He has taken iron and made something like bull horns. He somehow puts it up to his head and says, "With horns like this, you will push the Syrians. You'll gore them all. Hook them. You're going to destroy them."

About that time, Micaiah arrives. Ahab asks, "Are we going to win when we fight the Syrians?" Micaiah looks at all the prophets who have been saying, "You're going to win, you're going to win, you're going to win," and he mocks them, and he mocks the kings. He says, "Oh, yeah, yeah, yeah. You should go. Absolutely. You're going to win. These guys couldn't possibly have it wrong." Then, Ahab—not Jehoshaphat, but Ahab—says, "How many times must I adjure you, only tell me what God tells you to tell me." Ahab has had to deal with the wily, sarcastic Micaiah before, and he knows the prophet is mocking him. Micaiah then speaks the truth: "You're going to lose, and you're going to die. You want the truth? You're going to lose; the Syrians are going to beat you; you're going to die in battle. This is the end of you."

Then Zedekiah, the false prophet with the iron horns, steps up and slaps Micaiah in the face. He says, "OK, if you're a prophet, explain how the Holy Spirit was working in me to do that." Do those words sound familiar? Remember the trial of Jesus? When they hit Him, they shouted at Him, "Prophesy! Who hit you?"[4]

Micaiah then says to Zedekiah, "You will find out the truth of my prophecy when you're hiding from the Syrians in an inside chamber in your house." This must have terrified Zedekiah. "When you're hiding inside the safe room in your house, and the Syrians are crawling all over the city, you'll know that my prophecy, not yours, is real."

At that point, Ahab has had enough. "Seize him!" he orders. "Take him back to the city, lock him up in prison, and give him nothing but bread and water until I come." Now, I love what comes next. Micaiah, a tough little prophet who never cuts anyone any slack, turns to Ahab and says, "If you come back at all, I'm a false prophet."

Take note of this. Here's the number one difference between a true prophet and a false prophet. A true prophet says, "Hold me accountable." The false prophet says, "Forget what I prophesied when it doesn't happen." Micaiah, a true prophet, says, "If you come home at all, I'm a false prophet." Of course, Ahab is killed in that battle, and Micaiah's prophecy comes true.

———

Three hundred years later, just as the man of God prophesied, a man is born in Judah named Josiah, of the house of David. He begins a campaign of religious reform throughout all Judah. He rebuilds; he cleanses the Land of false idols; he tears down altars. He also brings the ark of the covenant back to the temple. He even moves outside the boundaries of his own nation, of Judah, and into the boundaries of the northern kingdom. He goes all the way up into Dan, way up in the north to Bethel. There he finds an old temple of Jeroboam's. He then turns to his people and says, "Here's what I want you to do. Go around to a bunch of the graves in the area and get the bones out of them and pile them up on this altar, and we're going to burn bones on this old altar."[5]

This really is shocking. Everyone in this story was an Israelite, and they were made unclean by anything that has touched death. Also, piling bones on that altar would spoil it forever. Still, they start going around and taking bones out of tombs. Then they come upon a double tomb with two skeletons in it. Josiah asks, "Whose tomb is this?" The people answer in Hebrew, *"Ha ish Elohim. Ha ish Elohim."* This means, "the man of God." They are the bones of the man of God that prophesied against this altar.

Josiah commands, "Leave it alone. Seal it up." Thus it becomes the tomb of the unknown prophet. Unknown perhaps to all but God. How amazing this is. God spoke a prophecy through this unnamed prophet, a prophecy against blasphemy and rebellion and idolatry that was fulfilled three hundred years later. This unknown prophet suffered death at the hands of a lion because of a stupid mistake, but it didn't invalidate his ministry. And at the end of it all, three hundred years later, God honored him. In Arlington, Virginia, we have the Tomb of the Unknown Soldier. Josiah, the good king of Judah, established the tomb of the unknown prophet.

LESSONS FROM OLD DR. MARK ABOUT FOUR KINGS AND SIX PROPHETS

Wait upon the Lord.

Sometimes the most strenuous discipline to which we must submit is waiting on God. You may someday face a great contest of wills with some powerful foe. This opponent may seem to have the upper hand, the strength and allies and resources that you lack. You may wade into that struggle with all your might, doing all you know to do, and it may still become obvious it won't be enough. That will be your testing moment, but it will not be a test of your strength or your ability to snatch from the jaws of defeat a strategic victory over a superior enemy. It will be a test of your faith to let God handle it, to release the outcome to Him and, most difficult of all, to wait—not just on His will but on His timing.

It is no small thing to speak the name of the Lord.

False prophets proliferate when the household of faith holds it a light thing to say "Thus saith the Lord." Predictions, political or historical, based on experience or wisdom, are one thing. Everyone can get it wrong occasionally; when we do, we can laugh at ourselves and move on, slightly humbled, to our next best guess. Prophesying in "the name of God" is another matter. Whether it is the outcome of elections, the rise and fall of nations, the undulations of the stock market, or who will win the Super Bowl, once you claim to have heard from God, the landscape of accountability changes radically. Now there's no shade, no rock of excuse to hide behind. Now you are out there, in the open, exposed and entirely committed.

CHAPTER 7

Elijah, Elisha, and a God of Power

*The L*ORD *heard Elijah's cry, and the boy's life returned to him, and he lived. Elijah gave him to his mother and said, "Look, your son is alive!" Then the woman said to Elijah, "Now I know that you are a man of God and that the word of the L*ORD *from your mouth is the truth."*

—1 Kings 17:22–24

I N 1924, IN Alexandria, Egypt, a Jewish baby was born. His name was Eliahu ben Shaoul Cohen, but he went by Eli—Eli Cohen. His family eventually immigrated— or "made Aliyah"—to Israel, but Eli stayed in Egypt to finish his degree. When the Egyptian government stepped up persecution against their Jewish citizens, he was eventually expelled from the country, and he too immigrated to Israel. Some years later, Eli began his work with Mossad, Israel's CIA.

Because he had been raised in Egypt, his Arabic was flawless. This allowed Mossad to create an entirely new identity for him, preparing him to infiltrate Israel's Arab enemies. Eli's leaders in Mossad moved him to Argentina and created a new life for him—fake name, passports, backstory—as a successful Syrian businessman raised in Argentina. From there he moved to Syria to begin his work as a spy.

His Arab alias was Kamel Amin Thaabet. He worked his way into the top levels of the Syrian army. Using his money and his charm, he also moved freely in the highest levels of Syrian politics. Once he earned the trust of the Syrian elite, he began sending intelligence to Mossad that changed the course of history in the Middle East.

The Syrian military leadership grew so comfortable with Eli that he was even given a tour of the Syrian military installations on the Golan Heights. Using his nearly perfect photographic memory, Eli carefully observed the installations and later drew the locations of every machine gun nest, pillbox, and artillery installation to pass on to Mossad.

In a famous story about this important intelligence

gathering, it is said that Thaabet, as the Syrians knew Eli, feigned concern for the Arab soldiers as a way to trick the Syrian strategists. He told the generals, "Look at your soldiers in these antiaircraft installations. They're out here in the broiling sun, and they're also highly visible from the air. Why don't you plant eucalyptus trees at all your installations so they'll shade the soldiers and hide the antiaircraft equipment from Israel's air force?" The Syrian military did as he suggested, but instead of hiding their installations, the trees marked those positions.

Eli continued to have stunning success until Russian agents deployed a radio tracking device that was able to pick up Eli's radio transmissions. He was captured, tried, and hanged in one of the most famous executions in Syrian history. His life is celebrated in Israel to this day.

In 1967, two years after Eli's death, the Six-Day War was fought. Israel won that war largely by decimating Syria's antiaircraft installations and winning complete control of the air. Many think this was a direct result of Eli's eucalyptus tree trick. It was a great victory for the Israel Defense Forces, but it was also the fruit of Eli Cohen's sacrifice.

Flashback 2,815 years, to another spy operation between the same two nations, the same two peoples—Israel and Syria. This earlier spy worked much as Eli Cohen did centuries later, bringing victory to Israel by revealing the plans of the Syrians. Both sides had their spies, but the chief spy of Israel was a supernatural spy.

Elijah was the great dean of the prophets. He was also the bane of the Syrian army. Elijah's protégé was Elisha, a gifted young man from a wealthy farming family. Elisha was chosen specifically by Elijah under God's direction. Elisha became Elijah's associate pastor, as it were, for seven or eight years, and subsequently his successor.

Consider the corollary between the relationship of Elijah and Elisha and that of Moses and Joshua. Moses selected, anointed, and ultimately handed over his leadership role to Joshua. Elijah selected, anointed, and ultimately handed over his leadership role to Elisha. When Moses led the people of Israel out of Egypt, they crossed the Red Sea, and when Joshua led the Hebrew people into Israel, they crossed the Jordan River. Therefore, both had supernatural crossings of a body of water.

Elijah and Elisha did as well. When Elijah sensed his life on earth was ending, he went with Elisha down to the Jordan River and struck the water with his mantle. The Jordan River opened, and Elisha walked through on dry land. After Elijah was taken into heaven, Elisha returned to the same riverbank, peering back across into Israel. Just as Elijah had done, Elisha struck the water, this time also crying out, "Where now is the LORD, the God of Elijah?"[1] And the water opened. Therefore, as Joshua crossed the Red Sea supernaturally following Moses, Elisha crossed the Jordan River following Elijah—miraculously, using nothing but his mantle. There are other such corollaries among the four men.

Take, for example, Elijah's "death." The basis of this book is the interaction between the prophets and the kings, but there is no way to arrive at Elisha's relationship with kings if we don't understand where Elisha came from.

As the story unfolds, Elisha is Elijah's second-in-command

and seldom mentioned. One day Elijah says, "I want you to stay here. I'm going over to the other side of the Jordan." Elisha, sensing what's happening, says, "Not on your life. I'm staying with you." They go down to Jericho, which is right on the bank of the Jordan River. Remember that the Hebrews entered the Promised Land at Jericho, and now Elijah is going back across the Jordan at Jericho and into a land called Moab. Again Elijah says to Elisha, "Stay here at Jericho. I'm going across the Jordan." Elisha says, "I'm coming with you." We must realize that these two tests of Elisha are not so dissimilar from tests in our own lives. To Elisha's credit, he senses the propitious moment. He knows what he should do. Always remember, there is a time to wait and there is a time to seize the moment. Elisha says, in essence, "I'm not sitting this one out. I'm coming with you." He seizes the moment. So they cross the Jordan River, and they go up into the mountains of Moab.

Once they are there, Elijah says again, "All right, I'm leaving. God has revealed it to me. My time here is over. Now, what do you want? What's your final request of me, Elisha?" The passage that follows in Hebrew is extremely complicated. The meaning in English is usually, "I want a double portion of your spirit." It may actually mean, "I want two-thirds." It could be that Elisha asked for two-thirds because he was thinking, "Hey, I know I'm not Elijah. I know I'm not ever going to be Elijah, but give me all that you can." So it could be a statement of humility.

However, let's work with the English. Elisha says, "I want a double portion of your spirit." Remember that according to Hebrew law, the firstborn son would get a double portion of the inheritance left by the father. So what Elisha seems to be saying to Elijah is, "I want to be the firstborn son of your prophetic ministry." This may sound arrogant on the surface: "I want to do twice what you do. I want to be twice as big as you are." That's not what he's saying. He is actually asking to be Elijah's son. He is boldly saying, "I want to be the firstborn fruit of your prophetic ministry. In that case, I get a double portion. Other prophets can share what's left over. I want the inheritance of the prophetic ministry that's mine, the portion of the firstborn son."

A question then: Can we say that Elisha was twice the prophet Elijah was? We cannot say this. However, we can come close to it if we look just at miracles. Elijah did work miracles, but Elisha actually worked twice the number of miracles in half the time. The two men have different styles. Elijah seems to be a "volcanic prophet." He kind of erupts from time to time. Elisha seems to work more steadily, more consistently, and at a more rapid pace—twice the miracles in half the time.

The comparison between the two men—Elijah and Elisha—is fascinating. Remember that it was Elijah who called down fire at Mount Carmel. This is typical of his nature and his ministry as we see it in Scripture: eruptive, volcanic, dramatic. Elisha, however, is more consistent, local, and relational. He interacts with the kings of both Syria and Israel. He also works intensely in Judah. He has been described as being "present," whereas Elijah is removed for long periods and then shows up suddenly for the power encounter, for what has been called the "miraculous eruption." Elisha, by contrast, travels around the country of Israel. He finds places of need and people who are hurting. In fact, people call out to him for help. Elisha is almost like a traveling evangelist who moves in tremendous supernatural power. A list of some of the miraculous moments in Elisha's ministry will give a sense of the dynamic he creates as he interacts with kings.

There are ten miracles that Elisha is known for. The first is the parting of the river Jordan on his return. That miracle we will encounter further on in this chapter. The second occurs when he arrives at the city of Jericho. The people there report to him, "Our water is no good. There's a spring here, but it's no good. It's fetid water, and we can't build a city here where there is bad water." Elisha then turns that bad water into good water. It is intriguing that his first "public" miracle is to turn bad water into good, a parallel to Jesus' first public miracle at Cana, when He turned water into wine. The parting of the Jordan, more of a "private" miracle for the prophets' eyes only, is more similar to Joshua than to Jesus.

Read the story:

Miracle 1—2 Kings 2:11–15;
Miracle 2—2 Kings 2:19–22;
Miracle 3—2 Kings 4:1–7;
Miracle 4—2 Kings 4:8–17;
Miracle 5—2 Kings 4:18–37;
Miracle 6—2 Kings 4:38–41;
Miracle 7—2 Kings 4:42–44;
Miracle 8—2 Kings 5;
Miracle 9—2 Kings 6:1–6;
Miracle 10—2 Kings 13:20–21.

Elisha's third miracle occurs when a widow asks him for help. Jewish tradition holds that she was the widow of the prophet who hid the priests of Jehovah during the reign of Ahab and Jezebel, but there is no mention of this in the biblical account. The Bible simply refers to her as a poor widow. Elisha tells her to gather glasses, bottles, and every container she can find and then pour oil into these vessels from her little vial of oil. Miraculously, she ends up filling every vessel. This is similar to the miracle celebrated at Hanukkah, in which oil for the lamps did not run out.

The fourth miracle Elisha performed was for the woman of Shunem. She and her husband cared for Elisha and provided for him. In response to their generosity, Elisha prophesies that she will have a baby, which she does. Again we see Elisha "on the ground," as it were. He's near the people. He's in the community and responding to the needs of those he meets.

Miracle number five relates to this same baby. Before the little boy is ready for his *bar mitzvah*—which means he was younger than thirteen years old—he dies of heat stroke in his father's field. Elisha then raises him from the dead.

It is interesting that Elisha is nearly always in contact with and surrounded by a group of prophets. In fact, they are involved in Elisha's sixth miracle. This group of prophets come to him and say that they have made some stew. Somehow, though, whoever went into the field to pick the mushrooms and other plants for the stew ended up picking something that was poisonous. Once this becomes known, Elisha takes some meal, a grain of some kind, and puts it into the stew, "healing it," as it were, of the presence of the poison. This is the prophet's sixth miracle.

In the seventh, we learn that there are a hundred men and all they have are "twenty loaves of barley bread" as it reads in the English Bible.[2] Now, we have to adjust our thinking here. When we read this, we tend to think of loaves of bread as we find them in a Western grocery store. That's not what the Bible is referring to. We should picture pita bread. This is the type of bread used in the Middle East to this day. So if there are twenty small, individual pitas but a hundred hungry men, there is a crisis. When this problem is brought to Elisha, he says, "Distribute the loaves, and there will be plenty for everybody and some left over." Once again, this miracle prefigures one performed by Jesus. Perhaps this feature of his ministry is part of his double portion from Elijah.

The eighth miracle is the healing of Naaman, which I'll describe a bit later. Naaman isn't a king, but he is a high-ranking general and represents a king. Therefore, I have included this episode as part of Elisha's gift for working with kings and high officials. It is also a testimony to Elisha's ongoing proximity to power. He always seemed to be with the rich and powerful in one way or another.

Miracle number nine is truly fascinating. The group of prophets approaches Elisha and inform him, "The Bible school is not big enough. We need more room." Apparently, Elisha is running a little Charismatic Bible college in the hills of Israel just as Samuel did. When the prophets inform him of their space problem, he instructs them, "OK, go cut down some trees and saw some lumber." Soon after, one of the prophets comes to him and says, "I was chopping a tree, and the head of the ax came off and went in the river." The man adds, "It was borrowed. And I don't have the money to pay this guy back." Immediately, Elisha takes a stick and throws it in the water. Amazingly, the ax head—an iron ax head!—surfaces and attaches to the stick. Elisha then picks up the stick and the ax head and returns it to the grateful prophet. Clearly, God is revealing here that though He established the laws of the universe—including that iron ax heads sink in water—He can override these laws anytime He chooses for the good of His people.

Finally, the tenth miracle is a supernatural moment involving Elisha after he died, giving us ten miracles associated with the ministry of Elisha—fully twice the number in the more volcanic, dramatic ministry of Elijah.

Back to the story. Elijah has indicated that he is about to depart this life, he has asked what Elisha wants from him, and Elisha has asked for the double portion that is due a son. During their journey to Moab, prophets had approached Elisha at Bethel and at Jericho, saying, "God has revealed to us your master is leaving." Both times Elisha says, "I know." He also tells them, "Keep your mouth shut. Don't say anything."

Elijah's departure is one of the more misunderstood—or at least misquoted—passages in the Bible. Keep in mind that Elisha has asked for the double portion and is told by Elijah, "You've asked for a double portion of the spirit that's upon me. What you've asked for is a really big thing. However, if you see me as I leave, God has granted it to you."

Elisha knows what is about to happen. Elijah is leaving. He does not know exactly when or how, but Elijah said, "If you see me leave, your prayers have been answered." Clearly the two men are standing together when a fiery chariot—a chariot of fire—and horses suddenly pass between Elijah and Elisha. We often hear it taught that Elijah gets in that chariot and rides off. Instead, the chariot comes between Elijah and Elisha, and Elijah goes up in a whirlwind.

What is happening there? I believe the chariot and the horses of fire represent two things. One is a separation. Those whom God chooses to take to His side, on to heaven, He takes as He chooses. The chariot represents that separation between the living and dead. Certainly, the fiery chariot separates the two prophets.

The second thing happening here is a test for Elisha. Obviously, a fiery chariot with fiery horses passing between two men is a huge distraction. Yet Elisha does as he must do to receive the blessing he has requested; he keeps his eyes on Elijah. This is a vital lesson for us. Don't be overly fascinated with supernatural phenomena. Keep your eye on the promise of God. Listen to what God has told you, and stay focused. Such remarkable "fiery chariot" moments are a blessing, but they are not to be our focus. Devote yourself to keeping your eyes on the promises of the living God and on the conditions of those promises.

Elisha is not distracted by the fiery chariot. He keeps his eyes where they should be, on Elijah. Elijah then goes up in a tornado, or a "whirlwind" as the English Bible states it.[3] As he rises in this great swirl, his mantle drops to the ground. Elisha picks it up. The message intended in this is clear. Elisha has "picked up" Elijah's anointing. The earthly ministry of Elijah is finished. Now Elisha's must begin.

Elisha now returns to the Jordan River. When he arrives, he finds the prophets who saw him leave standing on the other side of the river. This is a moment of great importance, and Elisha knows it. He takes the mantle he has received from Elijah and shouts, "Where now is the LORD, the God of Elijah?"[4] Then he strikes the waters with it. At that moment the Jordan River stands on end. This is only the fourth time in history that waters have parted at the command of a man of God. First Moses, then Joshua, then Elijah, and now Elisha. Therefore, Elisha is a full-fledged member of that great team of prophetic elites. It is the affirming moment and beginning of the wonderful, supernatural, international ministry of Elisha.

What comes next is a complicated, troubling episode. As Elisha leaves, a group of young men surround him. The English translation gives us the word *boys*, but the Hebrew allows for this word to be translated "young men." This makes a difference. An intimidating gang of nineteen-year-old men is a completely different and more threatening experience than ten-year-old boys. However we translate the word, these young males mock Elisha and tease him because he's bald. It is interesting that this is one of the only times in the Bible that we are given any insight into what a prophet looked like.

The young males start calling Elisha "baldy" and insulting him. Elisha puts a curse on them, and two female bears immediately come out of the woods and kill the young men—all forty-two of them.[5] Truly, this is a disturbing story. We might be tempted to call Elisha hypersensitive. Sure, he's being insulted, but it's just a bunch of guys teasing him, and this doesn't seem to warrant having them killed. I think more is being said to us here.

We should take the message of this moment seriously because a similar incident happens later in Elisha's ministry. When God says something twice, we should pay strict attention. The simple truth here is that God will not have His word or those who deliver His word mocked. We ought to think about this in the casual and sometimes borderline irreverent contemporary church culture. The young men mocked a man of God. They came under a curse as a result. This curse caused their protection to lift, and they were devoured by the forces of nature. This story is not about Elisha's petulance. It is about respect for God, His word and His prophets. May God restore respect to the church today.

Elisha's first encounter with a king is with Jehoram, king of the northern kingdom. Jehoram is the wicked son of Israel's wickedest king, Ahab. He rules from Samaria at the same time a good king, Jehoshaphat, is ruling Judah from his capital at Jerusalem. Both kings form an alliance with the king of Edom. These three kings plan to attack Moab because the Moabites, who are subject to the authority of Israel, had suddenly stopped paying a tribute every year.

It is interesting what the tribute actually is. The king of Moab was a master shepherd. He had many thousands of sheep, so each year he paid his tribute to Israel with sheep. When Ahab died and Jehoram came to the throne, the Moabites say, "OK, the old man's dead. We're not paying this boy." King Jehoram replies, "I'll teach you a lesson." So he covenants with Jehoshaphat and the king of Edom, and they march from Samaria down through Jerusalem to a place near the Dead Sea called Wadi Rum.

You may have seen Wadi Rum whether you know it or not. If you've seen the movie *Lawrence of Arabia*, you will remember the long, hot march made by Lawrence and his warriors through the desert. If so, you've seen Wadi Rum. I've been there several times, and it is incredibly hot. In that blazing desert, Jehoram's army soon begins to die of thirst.

Seeing the danger they are all in, Jehoshaphat asks, "Isn't there a prophet?" Jehoram replies, "Yes, Elisha." So they call Elisha out to the army camp. Picture the scene. There are thousands of men and even more horses and camels, out in the middle of the desert. Elisha approaches and the men cry out to him, "Can you help us?" Elisha looks at the king of Israel and says, "If it wasn't for the king of Judah who's here, I wouldn't even talk to you. I'd let you die in this desert. But Jehoshaphat's a good king, and so I'm going to help him. You just get to ride his coattails." That is not a respectful way to speak to a king, but everyone in the desert knew about those forty-two boys who were eaten by bears. No one wants to cross Elisha, especially when you desperately need his miraculous help.

The prophet tells the kings what to do. "Dig ditches all over this desert. Tomorrow when you wake up, the ditches will be full of water." What a perfect visual of faith in response to the word of God. What everyone in that massive army wanted was for Elisha to work an immediate miracle such as Elijah's on Mount Carmel. Elijah prayed, and God sent fire—immediately! They wanted Elisha to pray and God to send rain—immediately!

Instead, Elisha says, "Dig ditches." That's about the last thing they wanted to hear. They are exhausted, hot, and dehydrated. But they follow Elisha's directions and dig ditches. In fact, they fill the valley with ditches. That is obedient faith in action.

A rainstorm on the other end of the desert, at Edom, sends water coursing toward the ditches. They can't see it rain, they can't hear the thunder, and there is no lightning, but the water runs over the top of the ground in the desert because it can't soak in. A distant rainstorm fills all the ditches with water. When the Moabite army comes up over the top of the hill, the morning sun hits those ditches at an angle, and they seem red in color. The Moabites say, "Those three armies have turned on one another. The whole valley is full of blood!" So the Moabites put their swords in their scabbards and walk down to the desert floor to take their loot. They are assuming their enemies are all dead. Of course, they're *not* dead. Instead, the Israelites, Edomites, and Judeans pick up their swords and kill all the Moabites. It's a total victory in a single battle.

What does this teach us? First, when you need water and God says, "Dig ditches," then dig! Do the hard thing that comes with the word of the Lord, that often is a precondition of the promised blessing. Second, don't dig just once. This is a continuing motif in Elisha's ministry: be passionate, keep digging, and if you want more water, dig more ditches. Don't just stand in the middle of the desert and pray for rain—dig ditches. Third, keep in mind that the water came from Edom. It is a great truth that what God does elsewhere can affect what happens where you are. The reverse is also true. What God is doing in your life can affect somebody far away whom you don't know. There was nobody in the northern end of Edom who said, when rain started falling on their porch, "Man, this is going to work a miracle in the desert." There may be things that God is doing right where you are that will have tremendous effect on somebody far away. Fourth, God can provide for you and at the same time confuse the enemy of your soul. Notice that the only thing the three kings had asked for was water. God had higher purposes. He not only gave His people water but destroyed their enemies in the same act. Trust God to have more than one purpose for the things He does on your behalf.

Elisha's second encounter with a king is with the king of Syria, Ben-Hadad. He is a constant thorn in the side of Israel. The king's general, Naaman, was mentioned earlier and has leprosy. During one of Syria's many raids in Israel, a girl was captured who is now a slave in the house of Naaman.

This young Hebrew girl is the personal slave of Naaman's wife. She models faith and compassion even in bondage. Because she apparently has favor with her master, she says to him, "I wish my master, my owner, could go to Israel. There's a prophet there named Elisha and he will heal you." Ben-Hadad sends Naaman to the king of Israel along with forty camels loaded with treasure. He also sends a message saying, "Here is my servant, Naaman. He's got leprosy. Heal him."

Notice that he doesn't send this message to Elisha. He sends it to the wicked king of Israel. Clearly, he got the story wrong. When you need a miracle from God, be careful who you ask. The wicked king of Israel obviously could not help Naaman. In fact, the king nearly loses his mind out of fear: "This man is trying to start a war. He wants to fight! If I don't heal his man, this is going to..." At this moment Elisha steps in and says, "Calm down. It's me he wants. Send him to me." The king of Israel then sends a message to Ben-Hadad informing him that Elisha is standing by to help Naaman.

Naaman now goes to Elisha's house. Watch carefully how Elisha handles this moment. The most famous general of a foreign country arrives at Elisha's house hoping to be healed. Elisha doesn't even greet the general himself. Instead, he sends his second-in-command, Gehazi. Elisha doesn't even come out of his house. He instructs Gehazi to say to the general, "Go to the Jordan River and dunk yourself in the water seven times. You'll be fine." Gehazi does as he is told, and Naaman is understandably incensed.

"Are you kidding me? Are you kidding me? The River Pharpar runs right through Syria. Don't we have mighty rivers? What is this muddy little river in Israel? Is there something magical about this river?" Naaman continues his egotistical rant, "I thought at least he would come out and wave his hands around." Isn't this intriguing? Naaman is not so different from those today who care less about the genuine, authentic power of God than about a religious sideshow. What we want is a supernatural-seeming show. Naaman wanted somebody to come out and wave his hands around. Naaman would have been happy if Elisha had just waved his hands around, but it would have meant nothing. That's eerily contemporary.

Fortunately for Naaman, his assistants have wisdom for him. They say, "Look! If he had given you some huge quest, if he had told you to go kill some wild animal or defeat an army, wouldn't you have done it?" Naaman replies, "Yes!" So they said, "Then, try it. Dunk in the river seven times." Naaman does as they urge, and his leprosy is healed. In gratitude, he sends the treasure from King Ben-Hadad to

Elisha, but Elisha is a principled man. He replies, "I didn't do this for money, and I don't want your money."

While Naaman is returning to Syria, Gehazi runs after him. He says to Naaman, "Hey, my master sent me to you. And OK, like, see, he's changed his mind. And what he would like is, he'd like a little silver and a little gold and two Brooks Brothers suits. Forty-four long." Naaman, having been healed, is deeply grateful. "Anything! Take it, take it!" Gehazi then takes the treasure, returns to Elisha's house, and hides the goods in his own room.

Remarkably, Gehazi doesn't understand who he is dealing with in Elisha. The prophet says to him, "Look, if God would use me to heal leprosy, don't you think that He would reveal to me what you did? You want Naaman's treasure? You got it. You also have Naaman's leprosy." The immediate message is apparently, "Don't mess with Elisha." The broader principle is this: prophetic authority and power must be undergirded with character and integrity.

Following the Naaman incident, Elisha the healer becomes Elisha the supernatural spy! The king of Syria keeps trying to ambush and trap Israel's army.[6] God reveals this to Elisha. It's as though he's in the war room of the Syrians, hearing their exact plan. Elisha isn't in Syria. He's in the presence of God, listening. What he hears, he sends to the king. It's all very specific. "OK, don't go there. The Syrians are there." And again another time he says, "Don't go there, the Syrians are there." Finally, the king of Syria determines that since such specific information is reaching the enemy, one of his men must be a spy. When he accuses them of spying, they reply, "No, none of us is a spy. God is revealing our plans to Elisha in Israel, who's telling the king in Israel what's going on." At this, the Syrian king consults his spies in the courts of Israel. These spies confirm what the king has been told: Elisha is the problem.

The spying and counter-spying between Syria and Israel has gone on for three thousand years. Eli Cohen, Israel's secret agent in Syria, was part of it, but thousands of years before Eli was Elisha.

The king of Syria then realizes the source of his problem and he says, "OK then, quit trying to ambush Israel's army. Let's go get Elisha." So he dispatches his army to kill Elisha. The army's commanders consult the spies and ask, "Where is Elisha?" They reply, "He's at Dothan."

Under the cover of darkness, the Syrian army surrounds the small town of Dothan. They wait for the sun to rise the next morning, which is when they plan to attack. That morning Elisha's assistant wakes up and looks out the window. He says, "Oh, we're done for. We're surrounded." Elisha says, "What is it?" He says, "It's the Syrian army." Elisha says, "Don't worry. We have more than they do. There are more on our side than there are on their side."

The servant says, "No, see, you need to get out of the bed and come over here and look out the window, because there's like, not more of us. We're two, unarmed, and they are an army. We're surrounded." Elisha says, "No, I'm telling you, there are more with us than there are with them." So Elisha prays, "Lord, open his eyes." And the Lord does. Suddenly, the servant can see the vast army of angels before them.

Prophetic authority combined with the eyes of faith dispels all terror. Elisha is not terrified. He says, "No, we're surrounded by an angel army. They can't touch us." Elisha then prays for two opposite things. He first prays for his assistant to have sight, to see what is invisible to the natural eye. He then prays for the Syrian army not to have sight. He prays, "Lord, strike them all blind." So the entire Syrian army goes blind.

Elisha then does an amazing thing. He goes down to the enemy army and says, "OK, everybody quiet. I know you're blind. I'm going to help you. Follow me." He then leads the Syrian army into downtown Samaria, into the middle of the capital of Israel. Once there, he says, "OK, Lord, now open their eyes." When their eyes are open, they are horrified. The whole army is surrounded.

The king of Israel asks Elisha, "Should I kill them all?" Elisha's answer is yet another insight into his character. "When you capture prisoners of war, do you kill them?" The king says, "Well, no, I don't kill them." Elisha then replies, "Well, OK, these are not your prisoners of war; these are God's prisoners of war. If you wouldn't kill yours, what makes you think you ought to kill His? Feed them and send them home." So an undoubtedly shocked Syrian army returns home with their stomachs full.

Elisha's next encounter with a king is again with the king of Syria, Ben-Hadad. The Syrians besiege Samaria. They completely surround the city. The siege lasts so long that the people in Samaria are starving, and a ghastly thing happens. Two women are so near death from starvation that they make a bargain to cannibalize their children. They both have babies. One of the women offers her child first. They boil it and eat it. The second woman, though, can't go through with it. She refuses to offer her child to be eaten. In what must be one of the most disgusting lawsuits in history, the first woman sues the second woman for breach of promise.

The king is naturally horrified by all this when the case comes before him. He says, "Is this what's become of us? We're in such horrible shape that if we open our gates, the Syrians are going to kill and rape the whole town and burn Samaria to the ground. If we don't open up, our people will go on killing their own children." Calmly, Elisha says to the king, "Don't worry about a thing. This time tomorrow, you'll be able to buy a bushel of wheat for a couple of pennies. There will be food everywhere." One of the king's generals says, "If God should open the windows of heaven and pour it out, that couldn't happen."

In one of the most stunning miracles of the whole Bible, the next day God scatters the Syrian army. He does it by terrifying the Syrians with the sound of an attacking army overhead. There is no army, of course. There is just the sound of an army coming from the heavens. The Syrians say to themselves, "Israel has hired Hittite and Egyptian mercenaries, and they're attacking us from behind. The gates are going to open any minute, the army of Israel is going to come out and we'll be trapped." At this, the Syrian army flees the battlefield.

They are so terrorized that they leave their weapons and all their food right there on the battlefield. They also leave their treasure in their tents. There is so much food left behind that the king of Israel says to his general, "I need for you to oversee the distribution." As this general steps into the city gate to take charge of the distribution, the people are so hungry that they cannot hear him. Instead, they trample the man to death. This general who is trampled is also the man who said that Elisha's prophecy of God's provision could never happen. At that moment, Elisha said to him, "You say you won't see it? You will see it, but you won't eat a bite of it." And that's exactly what happens. The general is trampled before he can take a bite. Once again, a lesson from the ministry of Elisha: don't mess with a prophet of God. Beyond that, however, is this. Doubt and unbelief are the doorways to destruction.

There is a fascinating sidenote to the miracle where Elisha raised the child of a Shunammite woman from the dead. It also involves a king. Because there was a famine at the time, Elisha told the woman to go out into the country and remain there until the famine was over. When she returns, people have taken over her farm. She appeals to the king. Someone whispers into the king's ear, "This is the woman that Elisha helped." Immediately the king commands, "Give her farm back. And what is more, give her everything that you raised on her farm during the years she was gone. Pay her for all of it." This story reveals just how much esteem and authority Elisha commanded. The king rules completely in a foreign woman's favor simply because Elisha once helped her. Even the ungodly will respect a godly prophet of God. They may not treat him as honorably as Israel's king did Elisha. They may even want him dead. Deep within, however, the ungodly honor the godly.

Next, we read these simple, remarkable words: "And Elisha came to Damascus."[7] This may not seem that amazing on the surface, but consider that Damascus is the capital of Syria. Keep in mind that Elisha has repeatedly helped Israel defeat Syria. Yet we now find him in the capital. This must mean that Elisha's supernatural power and authority is so internationally respected that he can even walk into the camp of his darkest enemy.

The Syrian king, Ben-Hadad, is sick. He gives an order to his second-in-command, Hazael: "Go and ask Elisha if I'm going to recover from this sickness." Sometimes Elisha's prophecies are almost riddles. Remember that he said to a general that he would see the provision of God in delivering the people from a famine but that the general himself would not eat any of it. Elisha tells Hazael what message he is to give his king: "You will not die of this sickness, but you will not recover."

After Elisha gives Hazael this message, Elisha begins crying. Hazael asks, "Why are you crying?" Elisha says, "Because I can see what you're going to do to Israel." He then recounts what he has seen: "You're going to butcher Israel. You'll rip up the women that are pregnant with child, you'll kill the babies, smashing their heads on stones." Hazael says, "What are you talking about? What kind of a dog do you think I am that would do these things?" Elisha says, "You will be the next king of Syria. And you will attack Israel."

Hazael goes back to Ben-Hadad, says, "What did Elisha say? Will this disease kill me?" Hazael says, "No, the disease will not kill you." The next day Hazael places a wet towel on the king's face, smothering him to death. The king does not die of his disease, but he does not recover— just as Elisha prophesied.

In an episode soon after, God speaks to Elisha and tells him to do two things: "Go to Judah and anoint Jehu as the next king of Judah, and then go to Syria and anoint Hazael as the next king of Syria." I mention this because when Elijah was dying, these are the three things that God told Elijah to do: "Anoint Elisha as your second-in-command, anoint Jehu as the king of Israel, and anoint Hazael as the king of Syria." Elijah only did one of them. There's much argument about this episode. Was Elijah disobedient? Was he rebellious? Well, I believe he was old and tired. He took care of the succession of his own ministry, and then he said, "I can't deal with kings. Anoint the kings of two countries? No. I'm finished." Elisha finished the prophetic mandate of Elijah.

There is a final scene in the life of Elisha that moves me. It comes in the final days of Elisha's life. The great prophet is dying. He has surely been wearied and hurried to his death by all the great tragedies of the kings he has worked with. There have been many wars and murders and assassinations and treasonous plots and coups d'état. Now Joash is the king of Israel, and as Elisha is on his deathbed, Joash goes to see the great prophet.

Joash tells the prophet, "If you die, it's like the chariots and the horsemen of Israel are gone! You're more powerful than our army." Elisha says, "Take your bow and arrow, take it in your hand." Elisha then puts his old hand on the bow and on Joash's hand and says, "Now shoot an arrow out the window to the east." When he does, Elisha says, "You will win the battle at Aphek. You've shot in the direction of Aphek. You will beat the Syrians at Aphek."

He then says, "Now take the arrows that you have left and strike the floor." King Joash strikes the floor three times and hands the arrows to Elisha. Elisha says, "You fool! You fool! Now you will beat the Syrians in only three battles. You should have struck it on and on and on, five times, six times. Now you're going to win only three times."

When God is moving, do not settle for mere formality. Show some passion. Show some zeal. Attack! Elisha's final rebuke of a king was because the man did not show enough passion, enough zeal in pursuing the victories God had promised. Live out what God gives you with holy passion. Don't settle!

After Elisha died, his body was laid in a tomb. Sometime later, another man died. Just as the people of the village were carrying the dead body to be buried, Amalekite raiders were spotted heading toward the village. The people panicked and threw the dead body on Elisha's bones. So great was Elisha's power that even after death the man came back to life. The anointing on Elisha was so mighty that his bones worked a miracle of resurrection!

Who was this epic, transforming, unbelievably powerful Elisha? Prophet. Patriot. Miracle worker. Friend and foe of kings and generals. International secret agent and supernatural spy. Every prophecy he gave came true. After Elisha's death, Joash fought the Syrians at Aphek and beat them three times. God sees what we can't see. God can work what we cannot work; His supernatural realm transcends our natural realm. Truly, what a mighty God we serve.

LESSONS FROM OLD DR. MARK ABOUT ELIJAH AND ELISHA

Your life is measured by your legacy.

Your legacy is not how much of an estate you leave behind. It's not how many buildings you built or awards you earned or sports championships you won. Your legacy is the enduring fruit of your life, your impact on others for good and for God. It is your life's power to change the lives of others. A twelve-year veteran of the NFL, who once played on the winning team in a Super Bowl, was arrested for burglary and car theft. There is a difference, a huge and tragic difference, between winning a gaudy, diamond-studded ring and leaving a life's legacy.

When you consider what your legacy may be, when you evaluate not the successes and failures of your life but the impact of your life, don't think of what you've earned or learned. Think of Elisha's grave. When you're gone, will the effect of your life be life and power for others?

Among all the "Lessons From Old Dr. Mark" in this book, this is the most important. In fact, if you've read everything else in this book and missed this one lesson, you missed it all. Here it is.

Years ago when I was the president of a Christian university, I met a fine young man with whom I built something of a "hallway friendship." I always made it a point to spend some extra time talking to him when we encountered each other on campus. Finally, I asked him about his family. He told me he was the first person in his family to go to college and he was doing well, not great, but well enough, because he worked his heart out. He was not a gifted student, but he was a hardworking one.

I asked him about that one time. What motivated him? What made him work so hard? I will never forget his answer.

"President Rutland, my father drives a garbage truck so I can go to college, so I won't have to drive a garbage truck, so that my kids won't drive garbage trucks. That's why I work so hard."

And that—not a Super Bowl ring—is a legacy.

Ha Sof

*The L*ORD*, He is God! The L*ORD*, He is God!*

—1 Kings 18:39, NKJV

KING SOLOMON WROTE the following at the end of Ecclesiastes: "Let us hear the conclusion of the whole matter."[1] The Hebrew words translated "the conclusion," or *ha sof,* can mean "the end" as in the end of the world. *Sof* is even used in a fascinating Hebrew idiomatic expression for the middle of nowhere that translates literally "When you get to the end of the world, turn left." *Ha sof* can also mean more, as in the question "What conclusions can we draw from all this?"

After all, most of us are neither kings nor prophets. We are, however, what they were: humans who must live in the times in which we are born. These kings and the prophets with whom they dealt lived in times of great turmoil—just as we do. Their time held wars and rumors of wars, ruthless and evil politicians in high places, and religiosity without holiness. False prophets proliferated, and the true word of God was rarely heard in the Land. From the perversions of Sodom and Gomorrah to the idolatrous halls of Ahab and Jezebel, sin seemed so strong and the Lord's people so weak. The Land was surrounded by adversaries, and God's people were divided even to the point of civil war.

It all sounds eerily, disturbingly familiar. The principalities and powers of the present age seem so in control of this world, from the White House to the Kremlin. It *seems* that way. God is not disheartened or confused. He is not reading the newspaper to find out what is going on. History is not happening to God. It is unfolding in the palm of His hand. He is the God of history. He is also God in history.

Neither is His arm too short. He will not abandon us. He raised up Elijah and Elisha. He communed with Abram, and He summoned Moses from the deep desert and used him to shatter Egypt's might.

It is a historical naivete to believe that somehow civilization has gotten better. As the world was, it is. That is a hard word to hear and a hard one to say. Nations still rise and fall. Armies still invade. Cities are still sacked and burned, and peoples are led away captive. The world is as it was. That is the hard truth.

God is as He was and is as He shall be. He is I Am. That is the great truth. The God of Abraham and Elisha has not gone anywhere. He still has a people, a remnant who love Him. He can still raise up prophetic voices that will call us back from bondage and rebuke our overlords.

When Elijah prayed down fire on Mount Carmel, the people, who only the day before had been worshiping idols, cried, "The LORD, He is God! The LORD, He is God!"[2]

When all the kings of the earth are dead and gone and all the prophets are silent, what is the great conclusion of all the centuries of conflict between them? What are we to make of it all? Simply this: "The LORD, He is God! The LORD, He is God!"

Notes

Foreword

1. 1 Peter 3:15, NASB.
2. 2 Corinthians 5:20, NASB.
3. Proverbs 13:20, NASB.

Chapter 1:
The Counsel of God in the Muddle of Men

1. See Acts 11:27–30.
2. Acts 11:28, NASB.
3. C. Suetonius Tranquillus, "The Life of Claudius," in *The Lives of the Twelve Caesars*, trans. J. C. Rolfe (London: Loeb Classical Library, 1913–1914), accessed May 17, 2021, https://penelope.uchicago.edu/Thayer/E/Roman/Texts/Suetonius/12Caesars/Claudius*.html.
4. Acts 21:9, KJV.
5. John 1:29, KJV.
6. "Diary Entry: 26 May 1785," *The Diaries of George Washington, vol. 4, 1 September 1784–30 June 1786*, ed. Donald Jackson and Dorothy Twohig (Charlottesville, VA: University Press of Virginia, 1978), 145–146, Founders Online, National Archives, https://founders.archives.gov/documents/Washington/01-04-02-0002-0005-0025.
7. John Vickers, *Thomas Coke: Apostle of Methodism* (Eugene, OR: Wipf & Stock Publishers, 2013), 98.
8. Isaiah 6:1–8.
9. 1 Samuel 16:11.
10. 1 Samuel 16:12.

11. Isadore Twersky, "Rashi: French Religious Scholar," Encyclopedia Britannica Inc., accessed May 27, 2021, https://www.britannica.com/biography/Rashi.

12. Double AA, reply to "How Many Prophets Were There and Who Were They?," Mi Yodeya, December 22, 2012, https://judaism.stackexchange.com/questions/22946/how-many-prophets-were-there-and-who-were-they.

CHAPTER 2:
ABRAHAM: THE FIRST PROPHET?

1. Genesis 20:6–7, emphasis added.
2. See Genesis 14.
3. Genesis 13:12.
4. Luke 9:62.
5. Genesis 19:22.
6. Genesis 14:22–24.
7. 1 Samuel 15:33, KJV.
8. See 1 Kings 18:19.
9. See 2 Corinthians 10:1–5.
10. Genesis 14:18–20.
11. Hebrews 7:2.
12. Hebrews 7:1–3.
13. Hebrews 7:15–17.
14. Genesis 20:3.
15. See Genesis 26:1–11.
16. Genesis 15:13–16.
17. Genesis 15:17.
18. R. Richard Pustelniak, "The Blood Covenant," Beit Avanim Chaiot, October 1, 1994, https://www.bac2torah.com/covenant-Walk.htm.
19. Psalm 23:4, KJV.

CHAPTER 3:
MOSES AND A GOD OF DELIVERANCE

1. See Exodus 1:5.
2. Daniel 5:25–28.

CHAPTER 4:
SAMUEL AND THE KINGDOM OF ISRAEL

1. Sam Houston, "Speech at Brenham," in Amelia W. Williams and Eugene C. Barker, eds., *The Writings of Sam Houston, 1813–1863*, vol. 8 (Austin, TX: University of Texas Press, 1943), 295–300.
2. James L. Haley, *Sam Houston* (Norman, OK: University of Oklahoma Press, 2015), 450.
3. 1 Samuel 25:1, KJV.
4. 1 Samuel 2:1–2, ESV.
5. Luke 1:46–50, ESV.
6. Tamar Kadari, "Hannah: Midrash and Aggadah," Jewish Women's Archive, accessed May 28, 2021, https://jwa.org/encyclopedia/article/hannah-midrash-and-aggadah.
7. *Fiddler on the Roof*, directed by Norman Jewison (Los Angeles: Mirisch Production Company, 1971).
8. 1 Samuel 3:3–10.
9. 1 Samuel 4:7.
10. See 1 Samuel 4:9.
11. 1 Samuel 4:21.
12. 1 Samuel 3:19, ESV.
13. See 1 Samuel 10:21–22.
14. See 1 Samuel 13:7–14.
15. See 1 Samuel 15:22–23.
16. 1 Samuel 15:33, ESV.
17. William Shakespeare, *Macbeth*, eds. David Bevington and David Scott Kastan (United Kingdom: Bantam Books, 1988).
18. 1 Samuel 28:13, ESV.

CHAPTER 5:
NATHAN AND A KINGLY MESS

1. See 1 Chronicles 11.
2. 2 Samuel 12:7, KJV.
3. See 2 Samuel 7:13.
4. See 1 Samuel 9.
5. 1 Samuel 22:5.
6. See 1 Chronicles 21.

CHAPTER 6:
FOUR KINGS, SIX PROPHETS, AND A GOD ON THE MOVE

1. See 1 Kings 13:1–3.
2. John Wesley, *Wesley's Notes on the Bible—the Old Testament: First Samuel–Psalms*, ed. Anthony Uyl (Ontario, Canada: Devoted Publishing, 2017), 78.
3. 2 Corinthians 6:14, NKJV.
4. Luke 22:64.
5. See 2 Kings 23.

CHAPTER 7:
ELIJAH, ELISHA, AND A GOD OF POWER

1. 2 Kings 2:14.
2. 2 Kings 4:42.
3. 2 Kings 2:11.
4. 2 Kings 2:14.
5. See 2 Kings 2:23–24.
6. See 2 Kings 6.
7. 2 Kings 8:7, KJV.

HA SOF

1. Ecclesiastes 12:13, NKJV.
2. 1 Kings 18:39, NKJV.

All revenue & royalties from Dr. Rutland's books
go directly to support the ministry of

globalservants

**Please visit our website to find out more about
Global Servants and learn what you can do!**

globalservants.org

CONNECT WITH US!

@globalservants